CONSIDER THE
ISSUES

High-Intermediate Listening
and Critical Thinking Skills

Fourth Edition

Carol Numrich

In Cooperation with NPR®

Consider the Issues: High-Intermediate Listening and Critical Thinking Skills, Fourth Edition

Pearson Education, 10 Bank Street, White Plains, NY 10606

Staff credits: The people who made up the *Consider the Issues, Fourth Edition* team, representing editorial, production, design, and manufacturing are, Dave Dickey, Nancy Flaggman, Ann France, Amy McCormick, Lise Minovitz, Joan Poole, Jaimie Scanlon, and Katherine Sullivan.

Cover art: George Marks/Getty Images
Text composition: Rainbow Graphics
Text font: 11.5/13 Minion

Photo credits: Page 1 Shutterstock.com; **p. 2** Alexander Sandvoss/Alamy; **p. 17** Corbis Flirt/ Alamy; **p. 33** Shutterstock.com; **p. 45** Shutterstock.com; **p. 72** Courtesy of Prestige Photography by Lifetouch; **p. 75** Shutterstock.com; **p. 90** Shutterstock.com; **p. 104** Shutterstock.com; **p. 105** Gautier Stephane/Sagaphoto.com/Alamy; **p. 117** Jeremy Sutton-Hibbert/Alamy; **p. 120** Shutterstock. com; **p. 131** Shutterstock.com; **p. 143** Alexander Widding/Alamy; **p. 159** Shutterstock.com; **p. 167** Courtesy Everett Collection.

Illustration credits: Pages 9, 83, 169 Tracey Cataldo; **p. 160** Kenneth Batelman Illustration.

National Public Radio, NPR, *All Things Considered, Morning Edition* and their logos are registered and unregistered service marks of National Public Radio, Inc.

Library of Congress Cataloging-in-Publication Data
Numrich, Carol.
  Consider the issues: high-intermediate listening and critical thinking skills / Carol Numrich, in cooperation with National Public Radio. — 4th ed.
      p. cm.
  ISBN 0-13-231489-4
  1. English language—Textbooks for foreign speakers. 2. Current events—Problems, exercises, etc. 3. Critical thinking—Problems, exercises, etc. 4. Listening—Problems, exercises, etc. I. National Public Radio (U.S.) II. Title.
  PE1128.N8 2012
  428.3′4—dc23

                                                                2012020985

ISBN 13: 978-0-13-231489-3
ISBN 10: 0-13-231489-4

PEARSON ELT ON THE WEB

PearsonELT.com offers a wide range of classroom resources and professional development materials. Access course-specific websites, product information, and Pearson offices around the world.

Visit us at pearsonELT.com/issues

Printed in the United States of America
4 5 6 7 8 9 10—V011—16

CONTENTS

SCOPE AND SEQUENCE

USAGE	PRONUNCIATION	DISCOURSE ANALYSIS	FOLLOW-UP ACTIVITIES
Gerunds	/ŋ/: The sound in *-ing*	Quoting and Distancing	Survey: Social Networking
Separable Phrasal Verbs	Word Stress in Separable Phrasal Verbs	Register Shift	Survey: Cell Phone Courtesy
Antonyms	Rise/Fall of Intonation to Show Contrast	Turn-taking	Debate: Smoking in Public Places
Expressions of Contrast	Contrastive Stress	Referring to Prior Discourse	Interview: Working at Home
Negative Prefixes	Stress Changes with Prefixes	Discourse Markers	Case Study: Mickey Teubert
Present Unreal vs. Future Real Conditional	/ʊ/: The sound in *would*	Shifts in Footing	Case Study: Dial-a-Doc
Word Forms	Suffixes in Different Word Forms	Showing Objectivity	Debate: Is Marriage Necessary?
Past Unreal Conditional	Contracted Speech	Power and Roles in Discourse	Values Clarification: The Values of a Philanthropist
Noun Clauses in Subject Position	Thought Groups	Speaker's Stance	Values Clarification: International Waters
Parallel Structure	Listing Intonation	The Pronoun *They*	Oral Presentation: Biofoods
Compound Nouns	Stress in Compound Nouns	Jargon	Case Study: Chicago's Preparation for Climate Change
Superlative Forms	/ð/ and /θ/: The *th* sounds	Speed of Delivery	Oral Presentation: International Traffic Problems

INTRODUCTION

Consider the Issues: High-Intermediate Listening and Critical Thinking Skills consists of twelve authentic radio interviews and reports from National Public Radio. The broadcasts were taken from the programs, *All Things Considered and Morning Edition.*

Designed for high-intermediate to advanced English language learners, the text presents an integrated approach to developing listening comprehension and critical thinking skills. By using material produced for native speakers of English, the listening selections provide content that is interesting, relevant, and educational. At the same time, non-native speakers are exposed to unedited language, including the natural hesitations, redundancies, changes in speed, and various dialectal patterns that occur in everyday speech.

Each unit presents either an interview or a report about a controversial issue of international appeal. Students gain an understanding of American and international values and attitudes, as they develop their listening skills. Throughout each unit, students are encouraged to use the language and concepts presented in the listening selection and to reevaluate their points of view.

This fourth edition of *Consider the Issues* offers six new units based on broadcasts about compelling contemporary topics. In addition, *Looking at Language* now has three parts: *Usage*, which is grammar-focused, *Pronunciation*, which highlights pronunciation and intonation patterns relating to the grammar point in *Usage*, and a new *Discourse Analysis* section, which features a particular element of speech communication.

SUGGESTIONS FOR USE

The exercises are designed to stimulate interest by drawing on students' previous knowledge and opinions of the material, as well as aid comprehension through guided vocabulary and listening exercises. In a variety of discussion activities, students integrate new information and concepts from the listening material with previously held opinions.

I. Anticipating the Issue

Before listening to the audio, students are asked to read the title of the interview or report, look at a related image, and predict the content of the unit. They then draw upon their own knowledge or experience to answer questions and discuss some of the issues to be presented in the listening. It is likely that students will have different opinions, and the discussion may become quite lengthy, especially with a talkative class. It is recommended that the teacher limit this discussion to ten or fifteen minutes, so as not to exhaust the subject prior to the listening exercises. The teacher should also be aware that some students may be sensitive about some of the material discussed. It should be stressed that there is room for all opinions, but at the same time, students should not feel compelled to talk about something that may make them feel uncomfortable.

II. Vocabulary

The following tasks prepare students for new vocabulary and expressions used in the listening selection.

Vocabulary in a reading passage: Vocabulary is presented within the context of a reading passage, which also introduces ideas and provides background information to help students understand the broadcast. Students should read through the text once for global comprehension. Then, as they reread the text, they match the vocabulary items with definitions or synonyms. The meaning of the new words may be derived from context clues, from general knowledge of the language, or from the dictionary.

Vocabulary in sentences: Vocabulary is presented in sentences that connect to ideas in the listening selection. Context clues are provided in each sentence. Students should first try to guess the meaning of these words by supplying their own definition or another word that they think has a similar meaning. Although students may not be sure of the exact meaning, they should be encouraged to guess. This will lead them to a better understanding of the new words. Once they have tried to determine the meaning of these words through context, they can match the words with definitions or synonyms.

Vocabulary in context: Vocabulary is presented in short monologs, dialogs, or sentence combinations that are related to ideas in the listening selection. The vocabulary item is contained in the text. With the help of context clues, students choose the continuing line of speech. To do this, they must understand the content of the monolog, dialog, or sentence combination, as well as the meaning of the new word or phrase.

III. Listening

Listening for Main Ideas: The first time students hear the broadcast, they focus on the main ideas. Each interview or report has between four and five main ideas used to divide the selection into parts. Each part is followed by a beep on the audio. Only one listening is usually required for *Listening for Main Ideas*; however, some classes may need to listen twice in order to capture the important information.

In each unit, students are given questions or key words to guide them in comprehending the main ideas of the listening selection. Students are asked to write complete statements to express the main ideas. The teacher should stop the audio between sections to allow students time to write. Students may then compare their statements to see whether they have understood the main idea. The teacher may want to ask individual students to write their ideas on the board and discuss the ones that best represent the main idea of each section. Teachers may also ask why the incorrect answers do not represent main ideas.

Listening for Details: For the second listening, students focus on detailed information. The teacher should clarify any vocabulary or items that students do not understand. Then the teacher plays each part of the broadcast, stopping in between to give students time to write. Exercises may require students to complete missing information in sentences or answer true/false or multiple-choice questions as they listen, thus evaluating their comprehension. Finally, students compare answers in pairs. The teacher should encourage students to support their answers with information and examples from the listening. When there are disagreements over the answers, this discussion will help focus attention on the information needed to answer the questions correctly. By listening to each part a second time, students generally recognize the correct information. Once again, they should be asked to agree on their answers. If there are still misunderstandings, the audio can be played a third time, with the teacher verifying the answers and pointing out where the information is heard on the audio.

Listening and Making Inferences: For the final listening activity, students are asked to infer or interpret the attitudes, feelings, points of view, or intended meanings expressed in the broadcast. To do this, they focus on the speakers' tone of voice, stress and intonation patterns, and choice of language in specific excerpts of the broadcast. As inference can be subjective, students are likely to express slightly varied interpretations in their answers. This can be a starting point to an interesting discussion. For this reason, there are *suggested answers* in the Answer Key.

IV. Looking at Language

Usage: In this exercise, a specific language point from the listening selection is presented and analyzed in isolation, as a further aid to comprehension and oral production. A wide variety of grammatical and semantic points are presented. The Scope and Sequence on pages iv–v lists the usage points from the twelve units. Students are asked to listen to or read an excerpt from the listening selection and to focus on the use of the language in context. Then, through discussions and exercises, students apply the language point to different contexts. These exercises are not meant to be exhaustive but rather to help students be aware of a particular grammar or semantic point. The teacher may want to supplement this exercise with material from a grammar-based text.

Pronunciation: This exercise teaches a pronunciation point related to the language focus in *Usage*. Examples of intonation, stress and rhythm, and pronunciation are presented through audio excerpts from the listening. The pronunciation exercises serve as a further aid to comprehension and oral production. The Scope and Sequence on pages iv–v lists the pronunciation points from the twelve units.

Discourse Analysis: Like *Usage* and *Pronunciation*, *Discourse Analysis* highlights a particular feature of speech communication. Students analyze a segment of the broadcast to discover how speakers use language to create meaning, for example, by adopting roles, inserting opinions, or establishing distance. Then, through discussions and exercises, they practice the language feature in a different context. The Scope and Sequence on pages iv–v lists the discourse analysis points from the twelve units.

V. Follow-Up Activities

This section presents two activities. The teacher may choose to do one or both. Students should be encouraged to incorporate in their discussions the language and concepts from the preceding sections of the unit. It is expected that students will synthesize the information gathered from the broadcast with their own opinions.

Discussion questions: In groups, students discuss their answers to one or more questions. Students will most likely have different points of view, and should be encouraged to present their views to each other.

Oral production activities: Each activity begins with a note-taking exercise in which students listen again to the interview or report and note important details. By listening with a particular focus, students will be better prepared to complete the oral production activities that follow. The Scope and Sequence on pages iv–v lists the activities from the twelve units. In these activities, students solve problems and develop and express ideas while recycling the language and concepts in the interviews and reports. As students complete these activities, they have an opportunity to examine their beliefs about the issues presented. While each activity has a particular structure, there is ample opportunity for creativity and expanded discussion.

ACKNOWLEDGMENTS

I would first like to thank my colleagues at the American Language Program, Columbia University for their continued support of this textbook and in particular, Jane Kenefick, for piloting new material for the fourth edition of this book, and Linda Lane, for advising me in the development of the pronunciation activities. I would also like to thank Deborah Mowshowitz, Biology Professor at Columbia University for her helpful information on the bio-food industry. In developing content, I also received help from dear friends. Heartfelt thanks go to Anne vanKleeck for her insights into language acquisition and to Heidi and Wyatt Teubert for the contribution of their son Mickey's story.

My editors at Pearson Education were incredibly supportive throughout the development of this edition. My special gratitude goes to my development editor, Jaimie Scanlon. Her ability to refine tasks, simplify language, and find solutions is simply amazing. Thanks, also, to Arley Gray, who gave me helpful feedback in the initial stages of development. Amy McCormick and Lise Minovitz were also instrumental in providing the support I needed for the development and fruition of this fourth edition.

I am indebted to the many people at National Public Radio, who have continued to support this project from its inception. For this fourth edition, special thanks go to Wendy Blair for continuing to execute the fine production of *Consider the Issues* in NPR's studios. Wendy also, along with Frank Stasio and Daniel Zwerdling, provided the wonderful NPR voices for the audio.

Most of all, I am grateful to my husband, Eric Cooper, for having shared his unrelenting positive feedback and support of my work from the first edition of this book!

Carol Numrich

UNIT 1

You Have One Identity

I. ANTICIPATING THE ISSUE

Discuss your answers to the questions.

1. From the title and picture, what do you think the interview in this unit is about?

2. Do you use Facebook? If not, why not? If so, how often do you use it? What kinds of things do you post? Who do you "friend"?

3. In your experience, how have Facebook and other social networks changed people's social connections and relationships?

Read the text. Use the context to help you understand the meaning of the boldfaced words and phrases. Write the number of each word or phrase next to its meaning at the end of the text.

Mark Zuckerberg was born in White Plains, New York, on May 14, 1984. When he was a middle school student, he began developing computer programs, particularly games and communication tools. Zuckerberg attended Harvard University, where he cofounded Facebook with three classmates in February of 2004. He later dropped out of Harvard to run his company. Facebook achieved **(1) phenomenal** growth in a very short period of time and has had an average growth rate of 144 percent per year. Today Facebook's **(2) ubiquity** is undeniable. People of all ages from all over the world log onto their Facebook pages every day. Facebook is free, and until 2012, the social networking site **(3) monetized** its business solely through advertising.

Before Facebook went public, Zuckerberg had enjoyed a life of **(4) anonymity**, but he was soon forced to make public appearances because of the rapidly growing influence of his social networking site. He was named one of the top 100 "most influential people of the information age" and became America's youngest billionaire. But unlike most chief executive officers (CEOs), making money was never Zuckerberg's **(5) priority**. MTV, Microsoft, and Yahoo have all made offers from $1 million to $15 million to buy Facebook, but Zuckerberg has refused them all. He is more concerned with making the world a better, more open place, and he strongly believes in tearing down walls between people. His **(6) ethos**, as written on his own Facebook page, is "openness, making people share what's important to them." In other words, he would like to see people **(7) dispense with** their false professional or public faces, and become more honest about who they really are. He believes that Facebook is helping to tear down the **(8) façade** that many people put up in public; it is forcing more **(9) transparency** in our social world.

Zuckerberg and Facebook have not experienced success without some **(10) pushback**. Governments have threatened to ban Facebook in certain countries because they believe that certain groups use the site to spread **(11) sacrilegious** or offensive material. Zuckerberg's critics say that he is **(12) naïve** in thinking that people will become less concerned about their private lives. They argue that people will want to protect their privacy by presenting a public identity. His Harvard classmates, the Winklevoss twins, accused him of stealing their ideas and preventing them from developing their own site. Their suit won them $65 million in a settlement. Most of Zuckerberg's close friends who worked at Facebook in the beginning have left the company. The popular Hollywood film, *The Social Network,* portrayed Zuckerberg as a rather tragic antihero. It remains to be seen where Zuckerberg's young, powerful status will take him, and whether or not Facebook will continue to serve as the world's (13) **infrastructure** for social networking.

_____ a. convert into money

_____ b. lacking world experience and understanding

_____ c. being unknown or unacknowledged

_____ d. give up or get rid of

_____ e. extraordinary; outstanding

_____ f. resistance against something

_____ g. basic values or beliefs

_____ h. underlying foundation of an organization or system

_____ i. being everywhere at once

_____ j. a fake or dishonest cover, meant to hide the real thing

_____ k. not given the proper religious respect

_____ l. something important or necessary

_____ m. full honesty and openness

III. LISTENING

A. LISTENING FOR MAIN IDEAS

Listen to the interview. After each of the five parts, you will hear a beep. Answer the question in a complete sentence. Then compare your answers with those of another student.

Part 1 What kinds of issues has Facebook had to deal with?

_____

_____

Part 2 ▸ What does Mark Zuckerberg hope to achieve with Facebook?

_____

_____

Part 3 ▸ How does the author, David Kirkpatrick, say that Facebook will affect people's identity?

_____

_____

Part 4 ▸ How does Kirkpatrick believe people's attitudes toward privacy will change?

_____

_____

Part 5 ▸ What role does Kirkpatrick believe governments have in dealing with the Facebook phenomenon?

_____

_____

B. LISTENING FOR DETAILS

Read the questions for Part 1. Then listen to Part 1 again and circle the best answers. Compare your answers with those of another student. If your answers are different, listen again.

Part 1 ▸

1. What do many people know about Facebook?
   a. It was started by a 19-year-old.
   b. It was started by a freshman at Harvard.
   c. It was started by a Harvard history professor.

2. How many people now use Mark Zuckerberg's site?
   a. a half million
   b. one and a half million
   c. a half billion

3. What is the name of David Kirkpatrick's book?
   a. The Facebook Affect
   b. The Facebook "A" Fact
   c. The Facebook Effect

Repeat the same procedure for Parts 2–5.

Part 2

4. Where does Zuckerberg see the world opening up?
   a. on Facebook
   b. off Facebook
   c. on and off Facebook

5. According to Kirkpatrick, how is Facebook similar to life in a small town or village?
   a. People have more friends.
   b. People want to move to cities.
   c. People know each other's business.

6. How much do Americans use Facebook?
   a. Seven million people use it one hour a month.
   b. One hundred and twenty-five million people use it at least once a month.
   c. Five hundred million people use it seven hours a month.

7. How does Kirkpatrick say that Zuckerberg sees the money part of Facebook?
   a. Money is a priority.
   b. Ubiquity should come before money.
   c. It's not necessary to monetize Facebook.

NOTE: At the time of this report, Facebook was still not selling public shares on the stock market; however on February 1, 2012, it filed the paperwork for its initial public offering.

Part 3

8. What does Zuckerberg think about people having two personas?
   a. They can't have both.
   b. They can only have a professional face.
   c. They can only have a personal face.

9. What does Zuckerberg believe will be the result of having one identity?
   a. It may hurt him personally.
   b. It will be better for the world.
   c. It will cause people to develop a façade.

10. What is Kirkpatrick's opinion of people who put secret data about themselves on Facebook?
    a. They are responsible.
    b. They are naïve.
    c. They aren't going to be seen by others.

11. What is the biggest problem with privacy among Facebook users?
   a. scholars writing long papers
   b. peers sending quotes
   c. "friends" exposing data

Part 4

12. How is the Facebook community dealing with privacy?
   a. They determine what privacy is.
   b. They try to control the marketing.
   c. They stop doing so much digitally.

13. What does Kirkpatrick say happens when the quantity of data about us grows?
   a. It will be exposed in the world.
   b. It is less remarkable.
   c. It becomes problematic over time.

Part 5

14. What happened in Pakistan?
   a. The Pakistani government shut down Facebook.
   b. Facebook removed a group that was considered sacrilegious.
   c. Facebook violated its terms of service.

15. What does Kirkpatrick predict for Facebook's future?
   a. It will not avoid government pushback.
   b. It will stop the exposure of data.
   c. It will require users to have a passport.

C. LISTENING AND MAKING INFERENCES

Listen to the excerpts from the interview and answer the questions. Compare your answers with those of other students.

1. What does David Kirkpatrick think of Mark Zuckerberg's plan to build a social movement?

   _____

   _____

2. How certain is Kirkpatrick that people will continue to put data about themselves on the Internet?

   _____

   _____

3. Why does the interviewer say, "and not the U.S. government"?

_____

_____

IV. LOOKING AT LANGUAGE

A. USAGE: GERUNDS

Notice Listen to the following excerpts from the interview. Notice the boldfaced forms in each statement. What do they have in common?

Excerpt 1

And from the day he first created his system, he had this ethos **of sharing** that he strongly believed in.

Excerpt 2

So, there's a consequence **to having** one personality.

Explanation A gerund is the -*ing* form of a verb and functions as a noun. Gerunds can be used as subjects or objects. In the examples above, a gerund is used as the object of a preposition.

In negative sentences, ***not*** precedes the gerund. For example, in the negative, the second statement above would be written "So, there's a consequence to ***not*** having one personality."

Exercise 1

Work in pairs. Complete the sentences with a preposition and the gerund form of the verb in parentheses. Use negative gerunds when necessary.

1. Facebook users aren't used _____ _____ (think) about how their private information might be used against them.

2. Mark Zuckerberg is accustomed _____ _____ (share) information online.

3. He believes _____ _____ (have) two personas.

4. Employers sometimes take advantage _____

_____ (read) people's Facebook pages before hiring them.

5. Some people say they are not interested _____

_____ (have) hundreds of "friends" on a social networking site.

6. Are you capable _____ _____ (keep) in touch with so many people?

7. Facebook sometimes prevents certain groups _____

_____ (use) its services.

8. Some governments have participated _____

_____ (regulate) the Internet.

9. Zuckerberg looks forward _____ _____ (help) create a world in which we all have only one identity.

10. Being more interested in creating a social movement, Zuckerberg has

insisted _____ _____ _____ (worry) about making money.

Exercise 2

Write your own sentences about Facebook or other social networking sites. Use preposition + gerund combinations. The first one has been done for you. Choose from the word box.

be excited about	instead of
be guilty of	keep (someone) from
be responsible for	look forward to
be tired of	succeed in
have a reason for	take advantage of

1. *Instead of worrying about making a lot of money from Facebook, Mark Zuckerberg has focused on changing the way people share information.*

2. _____

_____

3. _____

_____

4. _____

_____

5. _____

_____

6. _____

_____

7. _____

_____

B. PRONUNCIATION: /ŋ/

Notice   Consider the pronunciation of *-ing* in the gerunds in the previous exercise. In which part of the mouth is the consonant sound /ŋ/ (ng) formed? Where is air released?

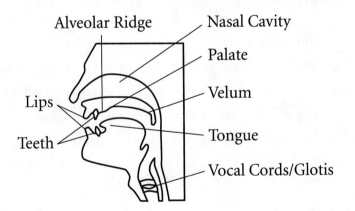

Explanation   For the pronunciation of /ŋ/, the back of the tongue rises up to touch the velum, or soft palate. The tip of the tongue is down, behind the bottom teeth. Air is released through the nose rather than the mouth. This sound differs from the other two nasal sounds: /m/, in which the lips close, and /n/, in which the tip of the tongue touches the alveolar ridge, behind the top teeth.

Exercise 1

Review the idioms and their meanings. You will practice pronouncing them with gerunds in Exercise 2.

bank on: depend on; rely on

cut down on: reduce

deal with: take action on something

focus on: pay attention to

get away with: not be punished for doing something wrong

get out of: not have to be responsible for doing something

give up: quit; stop doing

keep on: continue

look forward to: think of a future event with pleasure or excitement

put off: postpone; delay

put up with: endure something without complaining

think about: consider

turn down: refuse an offer

Exercise 2

Work in pairs. Read each situation. Student A asks the question. Student B responds using the idiom + a gerund. Practice the pronunciation of /ŋ/ in the gerund forms. Change roles after item 6. An example has been provided for you.

Example:

A: You're spending a lot of time on your Facebook page. What are you **thinking about**?

B: I'm **thinking about changing** the plans I made with my friends!

1. You are on Facebook too many hours a day. Will you ever **give up** using it?

2. You seem distracted from your work. What are you **focusing on**?

3. You failed the last exam. What do you need to **cut down on**?

4. You will soon take a vacation. What are you **looking forward to**?

5. The student talked to the teacher. What is he trying to **get out of**?

6. Facebook has grown so rapidly in a short time. What will it have to **deal with**?

Change roles.

7. Some parents never pay attention to what their children are doing. What do you think their kids are **getting away with**?

8. You canceled your presentation. What are you **putting off**?

9. Mark Zuckerberg's priority isn't building a business; it's building a social network. What is he **turning down**?

10. There are so many new postings on your Facebook page. How can you **put up with** getting so many messages?

11. If Facebook wants to continue growing, what must it **keep on** doing?

12. As Facebook continues to expand, what do you think Zuckerberg is **banking on**?

C. DISCOURSE ANALYSIS: QUOTING AND DISTANCING

Notice Listen to the excerpts from the interview. Why does David Kirkpatrick say, "quote, unquote"? What meaning does it add to the statements he reports?

Excerpt 1

The way he's always looked at it is, let's get ubiquity and once we do, then we'll figure out how to **quote-unquote** "monetize this thing."

Excerpt 2

And you probably also noticed that there's a—I quote a legal scholar who wrote a long paper last year in which he said he believes a large percentage of what we consider privacy problems with Facebook are what he calls peer-to-peer privacy violations, where our "friends," **quote-unquote**, are the ones exposing data about ourselves in ways that we don't like.

Explanation In written text, we can use quotation marks to indicate the words of another speaker. When people speak, however, it may not always be clear from their tone of voice that they are using the words of another speaker, so they may say, "quote-unquote" before or after the word or phrase. The examples above show each of these uses.

Speakers may also say, "quote-unquote" to distance themselves from the language used by another speaker. In the first example, David Kirkpatrick may be questioning the wording of Mark Zuckerberg in describing the goal of making a profit. Perhaps he thinks it is too casual a way to express such an important corporate goal. In the second example, Kirkpatrick seems to challenge the use of the word "friends" for people who would violate our privacy. Since Facebook uses the term "friend" to describe everyone with whom you communicate on their site, he may also be raising the issue of what it means to be a friend.

Exercise 1

Write three sentences to report something that David Kirkpatrick said in the following excerpts from the interview. Use quotation marks around any language from which you want to distance yourself. The first one has been done for you.

Yes, we live in an explosive world of data production and much of that data is about ourselves. And there's not much we can do about it with the extraordinary, you know, marketing apparatus that exists to try to target us both on and off the Internet, and we all just act so much digitally. We create data about ourselves at phenomenal rates.

So, you know, I think there's another side to it. There's a certain anonymity in obscurity. As the quantity of data about us grows, the fact that any given piece of data about us might be exposed in the world probably becomes less problematic over time. Because similar data is increasingly being exposed about everyone else we know—therefore it's less remarkable. And I think whether or not Facebook continues to grow, I think that's going to be the case. And we almost certainly will be less concerned about privacy more and more as time goes on.

1. *David Kirkpatrick says that it's interesting that a system which is all about "getting inside the business of your friends" has emerged at a time when we're all moving to cities.*

2. _____

_____

3. _____

_____

4. _____

_____

Exercise 2

Work in pairs. Take turns reading your sentences from Exercise 1. Say, "quote-unquote" before or after the language in quotation marks.

V. FOLLOW-UP ACTIVITIES

A. DISCUSSION QUESTIONS

Work in groups. Discuss your answers to the questions.

1. Some people believe that Facebook creates a false sense of friendship and actually makes it easier for people to avoid meeting people face-to-face. Do you agree or disagree?

2. Do you agree with Mark Zuckerberg's idea that we should work towards having only one identity and transparency, and that we should expect less privacy in the future?

3. Facebook has given individuals around the world the power to organize and create change in their societies. What are the pros and cons of this effect?

B. SURVEY: SOCIAL NETWORKING

1. Take Notes to Prepare

Mark Zuckerberg believes that as we share more information about ourselves, we will become more honest and less concerned about privacy. Taking notes on some of his ideas, as discussed by David Kirkpatrick, will prepare you to interpret public opinion about social networking.

Listen to the interview again. Take notes on issues raised by Kirkpatrick in his discussion of Zuckerberg and Facebook. Main topics and some examples have been provided for you.

Facebook's influence as a social network:

half a billion people use Facebook

_____

_____

Zuckerberg's philosophy:

world opening up

_____

_____

_____

Users spending time on Facebook:

125 million Americans use Facebook once a month

_____

_____

_____

Zuckerberg's business philosophy:

not building a business

_____

_____

_____

Two personas:

_____

_____

Consequences of putting secret data on the Internet:

_____

_____

_____

_____

How the idea of privacy will change:

_____

_____

_____

The role of governments:

_____

_____

_____

2. Write a Survey

Work in a group of four or five students. Using the chart on page 15, write five *yes/no* questions that ask people's opinions about social networking. Your group will interview a variety of people. Decide where and when you will conduct the survey, how many people you will question, who they will be (e.g., only Facebook users?), and so on.

3. Conduct Your Survey

Ask people your survey questions. Use the chart to tally the *yes* and *no* responses, and note any important comments that people make. An example has been provided for you.

QUESTIONS	YES	NO	COMMENTS
Do you think social networking has caused people to feel less concerned about privacy?	*/ /*	*/ / /*	*People just don't realize how their information is being used.*

4. Prepare to Present

Meet with your survey group to summarize your survey results. Prepare an oral presentation for the rest of the class. Include an introduction to your survey, a summary of the results you've gathered, and a conclusion including your own interpretation of your findings. Follow the Oral Presentation Procedures below.

Oral Presentation Procedures

1. The first student introduces the group and gives an introduction to the survey.

2. The next few students present one or two of the questions and the types of responses received. Be sure to share any interesting comments from the interviewees. The comments you share should help explain people's answers.

3. The last student concludes the presentation by summarizing the findings from the survey, interpreting them, and expressing the group's reaction to the results. (For example, "We were surprised to learn that most people thought . . . ") See list of Useful Words and Phrases on page 16.

Useful Words and Phrases

When you talk about the people who answered your survey, you can call them:

- interviewees
- respondents

When you report the information you gathered, you can begin:

- They agreed that . . .
- They felt that . . .
- They believed that . . .
- They stated that . . .

When you indicate the number of people who responded in a certain way, you can say:

- More than half agreed that . . .
- Less than a third said that . . .
- Over 50 percent of the group stated that . . .

"You Have One Identity" was first broadcast on Morning Edition, *June 10, 2010. The interviewer is Deborah Amos.*

A Courtesy Campaign

I. ANTICIPATING THE ISSUE

Discuss your answers to the questions.

1. From the title and picture, what do you think the report in this unit is about?

2. Do you think people ever use cell phones inappropriately? If so, give examples.

3. Should cell phone use be controlled in any way? If so, how and in which situations? By whom?

Read the mini-dialogues. Use the context to help you understand the meaning of the boldfaced words. Then circle the response that best fits the dialogue.

1. A: I can't believe that driver is passing me and talking on her cell phone!

   B: Yeah, especially since there's a law that **restricts** cell phone use while driving.

   A: _____
   a. I guess some people don't think they'll ever get caught.
   b. Well, I guess she's following the law.

2. A: Did you hear that guy's cell phone ringing during the movie?

   B: Was that the **shrill** sound I heard during the scary scene? I almost jumped out of my seat!

   A: _____
   a. That's a really pretty ringtone.
   b. Yeah, it sounded like someone was screaming.

3. A: I heard that a community in upstate New York **launched a campaign** to make it illegal to text while walking! They want to give out information and get public support for the plan.

   B: _____
   a. I'm so glad people are finally beginning to focus on the problem.
   b. I didn't realize there was a law against texting in that area.

4. A: I can't believe the way some drivers just cut in front of me on the highway.

   B: Yeah, they can be very rude! What's happened to the rules of **etiquette** in this world?

   A: _____
   a. Well, driving laws are different from state to state.
   b. People don't care about manners anymore, I guess.

5. A: I think cell phone users should try to be more polite when they are in public.

   B: Frankly, I don't **subscribe to** the idea that people can monitor their own behavior. I think they should be forced to change.

   A: _____
   a. So, you must think we need laws to control cell phone use.
   b. So, you must disagree with the proposed laws to control cell phone use.

6. A: I like the policies of that car company!

   B: Why? What makes them so different?

   A: They support good causes. Right now they are **sponsoring** a campaign to promote saving gas by taking public transportation to work.

   B: _____
      a. Doesn't that hurt their business?
      b. Why aren't they in favor of the campaign?

7. A: I hate hearing Dr. Long's cell phone ringing every few minutes.

   B: He should turn the sound off.

   A: Then, how would he know he's getting a call?

   B: Well, he could keep his phone in his pocket and set it on "**vibrate**."

   A: _____
      a. But he might not feel it when a call comes in.
      b. No, his answering service isn't very dependable.

8. A: I really enjoyed the concert last night!

   B: Yes, so did I. But wasn't that **disruptive** when someone's cell phone rang?

   A: _____
      a. Yes, it made me laugh, too.
      b. Yes, it certainly was disturbing.

9. A: I think it's great that more and more communities are making it illegal to drive while talking on cell phones.

   B: Maybe it'll help control some of the bad driving I've seen, but I'm afraid of a public **backlash**. People won't like it at all.

   A: Why do you think that?

   B: _____
      a. I don't know. People get angry when they feel they don't have a choice.
      b. Well, most people agree that cell phones are unsafe in cars.

10. A: Oh! There goes another driver on his cell phone. He almost hit someone!

    B: With drivers like that, I don't understand why so many people are opposed to **banning** the use of cell phones while driving.

    A: _____
       a. I guess they've seen too many dangerous drivers with cell phones.
       b. I guess they feel they should have the freedom to use a phone in their cars.

11. A: What have you decided about college?

   B: My parents are **urging** me to go to college right away, but I'm not sure what I want to study yet.

   A: _____

   a. They must not think education is important.
   b. Maybe you should tell them you need more time to decide.

12. A: What was the result of the town board meeting last night?

   B: It went well. For one thing, there was a **consensus** that the town should put more restrictions on cell phone use.

   A: _____

   a. What did they argue over?
   b. I'm amazed that people had the same opinion!

III.   LISTENING

A. LISTENING FOR MAIN IDEAS

Listen to the report. After each of the five parts, you will hear a beep. Write your answer to the question. Then compare your answers with those of another student.

Part 1   How is the city of San Diego reacting to cell phone complaints?

_____

_____

Part 2   How did people in San Diego respond to the survey on cell phone use?

_____

_____

Part 3   How have cell phone companies reacted to San Diego's campaign?

_____

_____

Part 4   According to Judith Martin, why is creating laws *not* the best approach to regulating cell phone use?

_____

_____

What is the challenge of Mayor Susan Golding's campaign?

_____

_____

B. LISTENING FOR DETAILS

Read the statements for Part 1. Then listen to Part 1 again and write _T_ (true) or _F_ (false). Compare your answers with those of another student. If your answers are different, listen again.

Part 1

_____ 1. According to this report, more than half of all American adults have wireless telephones.

_____ 2. People are buying cell phones at a rate of 46,000 a day.

_____ 3. Most American cities have restricted some use of wireless phones.

Repeat the same procedure for Parts 2–5.

Part 2

_____ 4. There are only a few places left where we aren't disturbed by cell phones.

_____ 5. Reverend Wendy Craig-Purcell doesn't mind when cell phones ring during her church service.

_____ 6. San Diego's mayor, Susan Golding, conducted an Internet survey on cell phone use.

_____ 7. As a result of the survey, the mayor decided to ban cell phone use in movie theaters.

_____ 8. Part of the courtesy campaign is to display stickers in "quiet zones."

_____ 9. Doug Cohen, a real estate broker, is against the use of cell phones.

_____ 10. Cohen believes that cell phone etiquette is similar to driving etiquette.

Part 3

_____ 11. San Diego is the home of many cell phone-related industries.

_____ 12. The Nokia company supports Mayor Golding's courtesy campaign.

_____ 13. The vice president of Nokia thinks that in certain places, people should use the "vibrate" function of cell phones rather than the ringer.

_____ 14. Cell phone companies don't know about the public backlash against cell phones.

_____ 15. Cell phone companies fear government regulation.

_____ 16. Cell phone companies urge their customers to drink responsibly.

_____ 17. According to Judith Martin, the "heavy hand of the law" is sometimes necessary to control people's cell phone use.

_____ 18. Martin believes people follow different rules when new technologies are introduced.

_____ 19. Martin believes about 50 percent of people know how to use cell phones appropriately.

_____ 20. At the news conference, the mayor's phone vibrates.

_____ 21. The mayor has trouble turning off her phone because she can't find it.

_____ 22. The Nokia vice president shows her how to turn off her phone.

C. LISTENING AND MAKING INFERENCES

Exercise 1

Listen to excerpts from the report. Listen to the speakers' tone of voice and choice of words. What is each person's opinion about public cell phone use? Take notes in the chart.

EXCERPT	INTERVIEWEE'S OPINION
1. Reverend Wendy Craig-Purcell	
2. Mayor Susan Golding	
3. Doug Cohen	
4. Larry Paulson	
5. Judith Martin	

Exercise 2

Using your notes from Exercise 1, rank the five speakers according to their acceptance toward inappropriate phone use. Write the number of each excerpt on the lines below, with the least accepting person on the left and the most accepting person on the right. Compare your answers with those of another student. If your answers are different, listen to the excerpts again to try and agree.

Least Accepting ⟵ — — — — — — ⟶ Most Accepting

____   ____   ____   ____   ____

IV.   LOOKING AT LANGUAGE

A. USAGE: SEPARABLE PHRASAL VERBS

Notice   Listen to the following excerpts from the report and read along. Notice the boldfaced phrases in these examples. How are they different?

Excerpt 1

Vice President Larry Paulson says customers should set their phones to vibrate rather than ring in certain settings and sometimes even **turn their telephones off**.

Excerpt 2

I think we will influence a lot of people to **turn off their cell phones** or to put them on "vibrate."

Explanation   Many verbs in English are composed of two words (verb + particle). For example:

turn + *off* = *turn off*

When these two words are combined, they have a new meaning. You cannot understand the meaning of these phrasal verbs just by knowing the meaning of the verb and the particle separately; they must be learned as a whole.

In some phrasal verbs, the verb and the particle are separable—they can be separated. In a sentence, the direct object can come between the verb and particle, or it can come after the verb and particle. For example, the phrasal verb "turn off" in the excerpts above is a separable phrasal verb. Notice that in the first excerpt above, the direct object, "their telephones," comes between the verb "turn" and the particle "off." In the second excerpt, the direct object "their cell phones" comes after the verb "turn off." The two parts of the phrasal verb are kept together.

NOTE: If a pronoun is the direct object of the sentence, it must come between the verb and preposition; it cannot come after. For example,

Correct: *Please turn it off.*

Incorrect: *Please turn off it.*

Exercise 1

Listen to the excerpts from the report. Underline the phrasal verb in each statement.

1. And with communities in Ohio and New Jersey already banning cell phone use behind the wheel, the industry may see a courtesy campaign as a way to head off further government regulation.

2. This doesn't even hang up well, but I want to be courteous and not answer it during this press conference.

3. The mayor later explained that hers was a new phone, and she hadn't figured out all the settings.

4. She got a quick lesson from the Nokia vice president in how to turn off the ringer.

Exercise 2

For excerpts 3 and 4 in Exercise 1, find the direct object of the phrasal verb. Rewrite the sentence on a separate piece of paper, placing the direct object between the verb and the preposition. An example has been provided for you.

Example:

And with communities in Ohio and New Jersey already banning cell phone use behind the wheel, the industry may see a courtesy campaign as a way to head off further government regulation.

And with communities in Ohio and New Jersey already banning cell phone

use behind the wheel, the industry may see a courtesy campaign as a way

*to **head government regulation off**.*

Exercise 3

Read the sentences. Then rewrite each sentence replacing the underlined phrase with the correct phrasal verb from the box. Find the direct object of the verb and draw an arrow to show how it can separate the phrasal verb. The first one has been done for you.

call up	tie up
give up	turn down
~~pick up~~	use up
switch off	

1. Most people like the convenience of having a cell phone. They can just <u>grab</u> the phone and place a call wherever they are.

   Most people like the convenience of having a cell phone. They can just pick up (the phone) and place a call wherever they are.

2. Although many people complain about others' cell phone use, few people are willing to <u>stop using</u> their own cell phones.

   _____

   _____

3. All the emergency calls had <u>clogged</u> the land lines, so the only way to reach his mother was with a cell phone.

   _____

   _____

4. One way to be more courteous with cell phones is to <u>lower the volume on</u> the ringer in public places.

   _____

   _____

5. Cell phone companies usually offer several minutes of free calling time each month, but it is easy to <u>spend</u> those free minutes if you like to talk on the phone a lot.

   _____

   _____

6. One advantage of having a cell phone in your car is that if you're caught in traffic, you can <u>telephone</u> your boss to tell him or her that you are running late.

   _____

   _____

7. The biggest challenge for teachers today is to get their students to <u>press "power off" on</u> their cell phones.

   _____

   _____

B. PRONUNCIATION: WORD STRESS IN SEPARABLE PHRASAL VERBS

Notice Listen to the following excerpts. Pay attention to the pronunciation of the phrasal verbs. Notice that the particle is stressed more.

Excerpt 1

And with communities in Ohio and New Jersey already banning cell phone use behind the wheel, the industry may see a courtesy campaign as a way to **head off** further government regulation.

Excerpt 2

This doesn't even **hang up** well. But I want to be courteous and not answer it during this press conference.

Excerpt 3

The mayor later explained that hers was a new phone, and she hadn't **figured out** all the settings.

Excerpt 4

She got a quick lesson from the Nokia vice president in how to **turn off** the ringer.

Explanation In separable phrasal verbs, like those in the examples above, the particle is stressed. The particle often receives even more stress when a pronoun comes between the verb and its particle. If pronouns replaced the objects in sentences 1, 3, and 4 above, the particles would be more heavily stressed:

   head it **OFF**   *figure them* **OUT**   *turn it* **OFF**

Exercise

Work in pairs. Complete each dialogue with the correct phrasal verb, separated by a pronoun. Then read the dialogue aloud. Be sure to stress the particle in the phrasal verb. Change roles after item 5. The first one has been done for you.

call off	head off	throw away
call up	put away	~~turn off~~
figure out	tie up	use up

   1. A: Brian's cell phone is so annoying in class!

      B: Yeah. The teacher should just tell him to ___*turn it off*___
          before he comes into the classroom.

2. A: I wonder how my parents are doing. I haven't talked to them in ages!

   B: Why don't you just _____ to see how they are?

3. A: My cell phone never works. The ringer is too quiet, and I can't always make calls when I want to.

   B: If I were you, I would just _____ and get a new one!

4. A: My girlfriend is always on her cell phone. She says she wants to spend more time with me, but whenever we go out, she's on the phone most of the evening!

   B: Ask her to _____ when you're with her.

5. A: I get a hundred free minutes from my cell phone company every month!

   B: Really? I would never be able to _____ since I rarely talk on the phone.

Change roles.

6. A: I can't get through to London. It seems that all the telephone lines are occupied.

   B: I can't imagine what would _____ at this hour!

7. A: Uh-oh! Here comes my boss. He gets angry when I use my cell phone at work.

   B: Don't worry. I'll try to _____ at the water fountain. Then he won't see you.

8. A: This new cell phone is so complicated. I read the instructions, but I can't seem to make it work.

   B: Here. Let me try to _____.

9. A: The meeting was scheduled for 7:30 tomorrow morning, but not everyone has confirmed that they are coming.

   B: Really? Maybe you should _____ and reschedule a meeting for a time when you know everyone will be there.

C. DISCOURSE ANALYSIS: REGISTER SHIFT

Notice   **Listen to the comment made by Judith Martin. What can you say about the way she speaks? Where does she shift her way of talking to speak to a different audience? What do you notice about the grammatical form she uses?**

Excerpt

If you use the heavy hand of the law for everyday trivial things, you create this state where everybody is angry at everybody else, where the courts are clogged up. This is a very simple thing we're talking about: Don't disturb people, you know. Don't talk at the movies. Don't talk on the phone in the movies. Don't talk to the person next to you in the movies.

Explanation   Judith Martin is an expert on manners. In the radio report, she gives her opinion about manners. Then she changes her voice and begins speaking in her role as "Miss Manners," giving advice to the general public.

     Notice that as she changes her voice, she begins to use the imperative mood. We use imperatives to give someone directions, or when we explain how to do something. As an "expert" on manners, Martin is in a position to tell people how to behave. The imperative mood is often used by people in a position of authority or power, such as when parents speak to their children or when employers speak to employees.

Exercise 1

Read the following imperative statements. In what situation might they be used? Match each statement with the correct situation. Compare your answers with those of another student.

Statement	Situation
_____ 1. Submit your papers by next Monday at the latest.	a. boss / employee
_____ 2. Clean your room, or you're not going out tonight.	b. doctor / patient
_____ 3. Don't park on the grass.	c. judge / courtroom
_____ 4. Mix the milk and butter together.	d. traffic officer / driver
_____ 5. Finish this report before you leave tonight.	e. teacher / students
_____ 6. Be seated.	f. parent / teenager
_____ 7. Take two of these tonight and call me in the morning.	g. recipe writer / cooks

Exercise 2

Imperatives can be expressed in different ways, depending on how strong or powerful the speaker's message is. Work in a group. Consider one of Judith Martin's pieces of advice ("Don't talk at the movies.") and rank it with other ways of expressing the same message. Write *1* for the least strong and *5* for the strongest.

_____ "Don't talk at the movies."

_____ "You had better not talk at the movies."

_____ "You should not talk at the movies."

_____ "It is not a good idea to talk at the movies."

_____ "Never talk at the movies."

Exercise 3

Practice using these other ways to express imperatives. Work in pairs. Take turns changing the statements in Exercise 1, using the following words and phrases. An example has been provided below.

> Always . . . / Never . . .
> It's a good idea to . . . / It's not a good idea to . . .
> You had better . . . / You had better not . . .
> You should . . . / You shouldn't . . .

Example:

You should submit your papers by Monday at the latest.

V. FOLLOW-UP ACTIVITIES

A. DISCUSSION QUESTIONS

Work in small groups. Discuss your answers to the questions.

1. Do you agree that many people have the attitude that "others shouldn't annoy them with their phones" but that "they don't necessarily apply the same rule to themselves"? Do people believe they are in "an etiquette-free zone" while using cell phones? Where do you see this attitude?

2. On a separate piece of paper, make a list of rules of etiquette that you think people should follow when using cell phones. List your rules according to specific places where cell phones are often used. Use the imperative mood.

B. SURVEY: CELL PHONE COURTESY

1. Take Notes to Prepare

San Diego has initiated an unusual campaign to encourage more cell phone courtesy. Taking notes on the specific complaints and proposed solutions to cell phone disruptions will prepare you to interpret public opinion about this issue.

Listen to the report again. Take notes on San Diego's courtesy campaign. Main topics and some examples have been provided for you. Use your notes to create questions for the survey that follows.

Places where cell phones are disturbing:

movie theaters,

_____

_____

People's complaints about cell phones:

disruptive in movie theaters

_____

_____

_____

Solutions proposed by San Diego's Mayor Susan Golding:

Post "quiet zone" stickers

_____

_____

_____

Problems with banning cell phone use:

_____

_____

_____

_____

2. Write a Survey

Work in a group of four or five students. Using the chart below, write five *yes/no* questions that ask people's opinions about cell phone courtesy. You might begin your questions with *Do you think . . . ?, Do you agree that . . . ?,* or *Would you support . . . ?*

Your group will interview a variety of people. They can be other students, teachers from your school, people in a train or bus station, etc. Decide where and when you will conduct the survey, how many people you will question, who they will be, etc.

3. Conduct Your Survey

Ask people your survey questions. Use the chart to tally the *yes* and *no* responses, and note any important comments that people make. An example has been provided for you.

QUESTIONS	YES	NO	COMMENTS
Do you think we need laws to control inappropriate cell phone use?	*/ /*	*/ / /*	*People never think that they are the problem.*

4. Prepare to Present

Meet with your survey group to summarize your survey results. Prepare an oral presentation for the rest of the class. Include an introduction to your survey, a summary of the results you have gathered, and a conclusion including your own interpretation of your findings. Follow the Oral Presentation Procedures below.

Oral Presentation Procedures

1. The first student introduces the group and gives an introduction to the survey.

2. The next few students present one or two of the questions and the types of responses received. Be sure to share any interesting comments from

the interviewees. The comments you share should help explain people's answers.

3. The last student concludes the presentation by summarizing the findings from the survey, interpreting them, and expressing the group's reaction to the results. (For example, "We were surprised to learn that most people thought . . . ")

Useful Words and Phrases

When you talk about the people who answered your survey, you can call them:

- interviewees
- respondents

When you report the information you gathered, you can begin:

- They agreed that . . .
- They felt that . . .
- They believed that . . .
- They stated that . . .

When you indicate the number of people who responded in a certain way, you can say:

- More than half agreed that . . .
- Less than a third said that . . .
- Over 50 percent of the group stated that . . .

"A Courtesy Campaign" was first broadcast on Morning Edition, *July 25, 2000. The reporter is Scott Horsley.*

UNIT 3

Give Me My Place to Smoke!

I. ANTICIPATING THE ISSUE

Discuss your answers to the questions.

1. From the title and picture, what do you think the interview in this unit is about?

2. Is smoking common in your country? What types of people (age, gender) typically smoke there?

3. Is smoking permitted in most public places in your country? Where is smoking restricted?

33

Exercise 1

Read the sentences. Use the context to help you understand the meaning of the boldfaced words and phrases. Then write a synonym or your own definition of the words and phrases.

1. We all know that smoking can lead to cancer and heart disease, but now it is clear that breathing **secondhand** smoke can, too.

   _____

   _____

2. Robin's parents always had strong opinions about government leaders, but Robin is really **apolitical**.

   _____

   _____

3. Gary loves to entertain his friends at home. He usually serves them a **cocktail** or soft drink before they sit down to dinner.

   _____

   _____

4. Erin is always on her cell phone, **blabbing** endlessly with her best friend.

   _____

   _____

5. The robbers moved **furtively** through the back door, hoping no one would see them.

   _____

   _____

6. In the 1940s and 1950s, people were generally not **cognizant** of the dangers of smoking.

   _____

   _____

7. Feeling nervous, Chris **took a drag** of his cigarette before answering each question during his telephone interview.

_____

_____

8. As there are so few public places that allow smoking nowadays, some smokers have begun to feel **defiance**.

_____

_____

9. Jordan was not aware of the pain he had **inflicted** on his parents during his teenage years.

_____

_____

10. They need a stronger **patrol** around these prison walls; some prisoners have actually escaped!

_____

_____

11. After hours of questioning, the accused man finally **knuckled under** and told the truth about the crime he had committed.

_____

_____

Exercise 2

Match the words on the left to their definitions on the right.

	Words		Definitions
_____	1. secondhand	a.	inhale smoke from a cigarette
_____	2. apolitical	b.	talking foolishly and too much
_____	3. cocktail	c.	secretively
_____	4. blabbing	d.	impose
_____	5. furtively	e.	not direct from the original source
_____	6. cognizant	f.	politically disinterested
_____	7. take a drag	g.	police; guard
_____	8. defiance	h.	resistance
_____	9. inflict	i.	give up; give in to pressure
_____	10. patrol	j.	mixed alcoholic beverage
_____	11. knuckle under	k.	aware

A. LISTENING FOR MAIN IDEAS

Listen to the report. After each of the five parts, you will hear a beep. Write your answer to the question in a complete sentence. Then compare your answers with those of another student.

Part 1   What has changed about smoking over the years?

_____

_____

Part 2   How have smokers changed their behavior in people's homes?

_____

_____

Part 3   How have smokers changed their habits?

_____

_____

Part 4   In what situations do smokers feel defiance?

_____

_____

Part 5   How do Michael and Peggy react differently toward people's feelings about smoking?

_____

_____

B. LISTENING FOR DETAILS

Read the statements for Part 1. Then listen to Part 1 again and write *T* (true) or *F* (false). Compare your answers with those of another student. If your answers are different, listen again.

Part 1

_____ 1. Peggy has smoked for over 35 years.

_____ 2. Peggy and Michael feel comfortable smoking in their neighborhood bar in Washington, D.C.

_____ 3. The EPA[1] report on secondhand smoke[2] will restrict smoking in public places.

_____ 4. Peggy gave more thought to her smoking 35 years ago.

_____ 5. Peggy thinks today's attitude toward smoking is similar to other attitudes toward freedom.

Repeat the same procedure for Parts 2–5.

Part 2

_____ 6. According to Michael, 15 years ago, people usually offered him an ashtray when he visited their homes.

_____ 7. Michael says that people used to drink, smoke, and talk at the same time at parties.

_____ 8. Now smokers often have to stand at the window or outside the house.

Part 3

_____ 9. Peggy never lights up a cigarette in someone's office or home.

_____ 10. In a group, Michael now blows his smoke straight toward the other people.

_____ 11. Michael thinks he looks like a factory when he smokes.

Part 4

_____ 12. Michael has sometimes felt a desire to inflict his habit on others.

_____ 13. Michael feels defiance when someone doesn't want him to smoke in a place where smoking is allowed.

_____ 14. Michael believed that the man behind him was really bothered physically by the man's smoke.

_____ 15. Peggy feels defiance when others judge her behavior.

---

[1]*Environmental Protection Agency:* This means that the report was government funded.
[2]*secondhand smoke:* smoke exhaled by a smoker that is inhaled by another person

_____ 16. Michael can understand people who don't want to be around smoke.

_____ 17. Michael follows the antismoking rules.

_____ 18. Peggy would only consider going to restaurants that allow smoking.

_____ 19. Peggy feels smokers should have the same rights as nonsmokers.

C. LISTENING AND MAKING INFERENCES

Listen to the excerpts and answer the questions. Compare your answers with those of other students.

1. What is Peggy's opinion of smoking's lack of popularity?
   a. It is political.
   b. It is apolitical.
   c. It may or may not be political.

2. Does Michael feel uncomfortable if he is told not to smoke in someone's house?
   a. Yes, definitely.
   b. No, not at all.
   c. Probably a little.

3. Why does Peggy mention the "fur patrol"?
   a. She feels people who judge smoking judge everything, including people who wear fur coats.
   b. She feels people think only rich people who wear fur coats smoke.
   c. She feels people think you're like an animal if you smoke.

IV. LOOKING AT LANGUAGE

A. USAGE: ANTONYMS

Notice **Listen to the following excerpt from the interview. Pay attention to the boldfaced words. How are these words related?**

Excerpt

And I don't know how much of that is basically **political** and how much is **apolitical**.

Explanation Like other languages, English is filled with antonyms: words that have opposite meanings. In the example on page 38, the antonym of *political, apolitical,* is formed by adding the negative prefix *a-*. Many words in English form antonyms by adding a negative prefix. Antonyms of other words from the interview can be formed by adding the negative prefix *un-*:

comfortable	→	uncomfortable
aware	→	unaware
acceptable	→	unacceptable
popular	→	unpopular
common	→	uncommon

However, many antonyms come from a completely different word. For example, *rare* is another antonym for *common*; the two words do not come from the same root, yet they are still antonyms. To show contrasts or give opposite choices, like in the excerpt above, it is helpful to know English antonyms. Studying words with these opposite relationships can also help improve our memory of new vocabulary.

Exercise

Complete the sentences with antonyms from the box.

cheerful	lose
deter	naïve
flexible	outside
forbid	public
gain	uncommon
hinder	unite
impolite	unpopular

1. Is it common or _____ to see a woman smoking in your country?

2. Does an actor who smokes in a film improve or _____ his image?

3. Do you think stricter laws against public smoking will divide or _____ people?

4. Do people tend to smoke more when they feel gloomy or _____?

5. Where are the smoking areas for people who work in this building? Inside or _____?

6. If I started smoking, would I lose weight or _____ it?

7. If the restaurant bans smoking, will it attract or _____ customers?

8. Do you think people look more _____ or more sophisticated while smoking a cigarette?

9. If your roommate started to smoke, would you permit him to smoke in the house, or would you _____ him?

10. When guests come to dinner, is it polite or _____ for them to ask if they can smoke?

11. Do you think the smoking laws here are too rigid, or too

    _____?

12. Do anti-smoking ads _____ people from taking up smoking or cause them to start?

13. Do you feel equally comfortable smoking in private and in

    _____?

14. Is smoking popular or _____ among young people in your country?

B. PRONUNCIATION: RISE / FALL OF INTONATION TO SHOW CONTRAST

Notice   Listen again to the excerpt from Part A. Pay attention to the two boldfaced parts of the statement. Notice the intonation pattern for each part. Which one falls? Which one rises?

Excerpt

And I don't know how much of that **is basically political** and how much

is apolitical.

Explanation   Statements or questions that give two options or choices have a rise / fall intonation pattern. The rising intonation on the first choice indicates that there is more to come. The falling intonation pattern on the second choice indicates that both choices have been presented.

Exercise 1

Work in pairs. Look at the antonym exercise in Part A on page 39. Read the choice questions to your partner, focusing on the rise / fall pattern. Your partner should answer the questions with his or her own ideas. Change roles after item 7.

Exercise 2

On a separate piece of paper, write five choice questions about smoking. Then work in pairs. Take turns asking your questions. Be sure to focus on the rise / fall intonation in your choices.

C. DISCOURSE ANALYSIS: TURN TAKING

Notice   Listen to the following excerpt from the interview and read along. Focus on who asks questions, who answers, and how the focus of the conversation continues or changes. How do the speakers share the conversation?

Michael: Well, 15 years ago you didn't think about it. You walked into someone's house, and they would offer you an ashtray. You don't do that anymore. I don't even ask anymore, "Is it OK if we smoke?" because for a while there it was, "Well, I really wish you wouldn't."

Kate Davis: And that was awkward?

Michael: No, it wasn't awkward; it's just you learn not to ask anymore, and just assume that it's not right.

Peggy: I found it awkward.

Michael: You go to parties now, and you know, where it used to be that everybody would be standing around with a cocktail in one hand and a cigarette in the other and blabbing, and now you see the smokers, kind of . . . if it's an apartment, furtively standing around an open window, or if it's a house, standing outside in little groups. It's pretty common.

Davis: Has it changed your smoking habits in any way?

Explanation   Turn-taking is an important part of building a conversation. In the excerpt you just listened to, Peggy tries to give her opinion about whether or not it is "awkward" when someone asks you not to smoke. She disagrees with Michael and does find it "awkward." Instead of following up on her opinion, however, Michael takes another turn and shifts the conversation to describe behavior at today's parties. When he is finished, the interviewer then moves on to another topic. Peggy has lost her turn.

Just like at traffic intersections, where drivers know to take turns in moving ahead, speakers in a conversation know to take turns in moving the conversation forward. Sometimes the rules of turn-taking are ignored, for example, when another speaker interrupts or changes the topic.

Exercise

Work in groups. Read the statements. Do you agree or disagree? Mark each one *A* (agree) or *D* (disagree). Then compare your answers with those of other students. Give examples from your own experience to support your view.

_____ 1. Not all cultures practice the same turn-taking rules in conversation.

_____ 2. Turn-taking is determined by whether one is male or female.

_____ 3. Turn-taking is determined by positions of authority.

_____ 4. People should never talk over each other; they should wait until a person has finished speaking before they speak.

_____ 5. Turn-taking is difficult to master when you are communicating in a second language.

V. FOLLOW-UP ACTIVITIES

A. DISCUSSION QUESTIONS

Work in small groups. Discuss your answers to the questions.

1. Should cigarette smoking be permitted in public places? If so, in which places?

2. Are the smoking restrictions in the United States unique, or are other countries changing laws on public smoking? Give examples.

3. Do you think tobacco should be classified as a drug?

B. DEBATE: SMOKING IN PUBLIC PLACES

1. Take Notes to Prepare

Comparing past attitudes toward smoking to those of today will prepare you to conduct a debate in the exercise that follows.

Listen to the interview again. Take notes on how attitudes toward smoking have changed over the years. Main topics and some examples have been provided for you.

	YEARS AGO	TODAY
Smokers' attitudes toward their smoking	*didn't give a lot of thought to it*	*keenly aware of other's perceptions* *realize it's much less popular*

	YEARS AGO	TODAY
Smoking at people's homes		
Smoking at parties		
Smokers' habits		

2. Consider the Issue

Divide into two teams to debate smoking in public places. Use your notes from Step 1 to help you prepare your argument.

Team A will argue in favor of smoking in public places.

You believe that smokers have the right to smoke in public places. You will argue in favor of providing smoking sections in restaurants, theaters, on public transportation, etc., so that smokers can have the opportunity to smoke if they wish.

Team B will argue against smoking in public places.

You believe that smokers should not have the right to smoke in public places. You will argue in favor of prohibiting smoking in restaurants, theaters, on public transportation, etc.; because you feel it is unpleasant and unhealthy for nonsmokers even when people smoke in designated areas.

3. Debate the Issue

Choose a moderator to lead the debate. The moderator will time the presentations and keep order during the debate. Follow the Debate Procedures below.

Debate Procedures

Preparation:

a. Each team meets separately to prepare a list of points to support its argument. (You may want to plan which team member will present which argument during the debate.)

b. Each team tries to predict arguments that the other team will make; then it finds arguments against each of these.

Debate:

    c. Team A and Team B sit facing each other. The moderator sits off to the side. (You may want to set a time frame for the whole debate.)

    d. The moderator begins the debate by asking one of the teams to introduce the issue and present the first argument in one minute or less.

    e A member of the opposing team responds in one minute or less. This back-and-forth format continues. After a member of one team has spoken, only a member of the opposing team may respond. Two members of the same team may not make arguments one after the other.

Wrap Up:

    f. The moderator announces when there are two minutes remaining, giving each team one final chance to make an argument.

    g. At the end of the debate, the moderator evaluates the strength of each team's arguments.

"Give Me My Place to Smoke!" *was first broadcast on* All Things Considered, *January 9, 1993. The interviewer is Katie Davis.*

What's Happening to Home?

I.   ANTICIPATING THE ISSUE

Discuss your answers to the questions.

1. From the title and the picture, discuss what you think the interview in this unit is about.

2. What is the meaning of "home" to you? What feelings do you get when you think of "home"?

3. How has technology changed the world of work and home? Give examples. Are the changes more positive or more negative, in your opinion?

45

Read the sentences in the box. Then read the numbered sentences below. After each numbered sentence, write the sentence from the box that best fits. Use a dictionary if necessary. The first one has been done for you.

In that **refuge**, they were protected.

Every day more cultures mix in this type of **fusion**.

It's a **phenomenon** that's sure to be seen more and more over time.

It's unclear and a bit of a **blur**.

~~That was a **eureka moment** that changed my life.~~

The water was **seeping** into our tent through the wet ground.

The sink had been **leaking** for days.

Look, it's **bleeding through** and making a mark on the table.

We need to set some sort of **boundary** to limit his visits.

This little piece of technology is the world's favorite **gadget**!

She always finds herself in **dilemmas**.

1. I'll never forget when I finally learned how to drive a car. *That was a eureka moment that changed my life.*

2. When I got home from vacation, my bathroom was flooded! _____

   _____

   _____

3. Increased immigration has brought new combinations of ethnic foods and

   international music. _____

   _____

   _____

4. I can't see where the sky begins and where the horizon ends in this

   painting. _____

   _____

   _____

5. These days everybody seems to be sending text messages on their
smartphones! _____

_____

_____

6. Mara can't decide whether to go back to work or quit her job and stay home
with the children. _____

_____

_____

7. Josh stops by to see us almost every night just when we're sitting down to
dinner! _____

_____

_____

8. The climbers moved down the mountain to a small cave before the
dangerous storm arrived. _____

_____

_____

9. You shouldn't have put the tomato in that paper napkin. _____

_____

_____

10. These days, more and more people are staying home to work. _____

_____

_____

11. It never stopped raining the whole night. _____

_____

_____

A. LISTENING FOR MAIN IDEAS

Listen to the interview. After each of the four parts, you will hear a beep. Write the main idea in a complete sentence, using the key word or phrase given. Then compare your sentences with those of another student. The first one has been done for you.

Part 1 ▶ fusion

Modern technology has led to new issues in the fusion of work and home.

_____

Part 2 ▶ blurring lines

_____

_____

Part 3 ▶ boundaries

_____

_____

Part 4 ▶ refuge

_____

_____

B. LISTENING FOR DETAILS

Read the sentences for Part 1. Listen to Part 1 again and fill in the blanks with the missing information. Compare your answers with those of another student. If your answers are different, listen again.

Part 1 ▶

1. The reporter, Liane Hansen, has turned her daughter's bedroom into

   a(n) _____.

2. In *What's Happening to Home?* Maggie Jackson explores the issue of

   balancing work, _____, and _____ in the
   information age.

3. The fusion of work and home in earlier centuries is illustrated by the fact

that many families _____.

Repeat the same procedure for Parts 2–4.

Part 2

4. With technology, our bodies can be _____, but our minds

are in a(n) _____.

5. With this fusion of work and home, you have a different relationship with

the people at home because you are doing work that _____.

6. The lines between Jackson's work and home life were blurred when she

hurried her kids to bed so that she could _____.

7. One positive effect of working at home for Jackson was that she could

interview _____ while living on the East Coast.

8. The negative effect it had on her was that her work was

_____ and _____ and _____ into
the rest of her house.

Part 3

9. Hansen says that the advantages of working at home for her are that she can
have a cup of coffee, sit in an armchair, and look at

_____.

10. Hansen can _____ to set a physical boundary between her office
and the rest of her home.

11. Jackson thinks that boundary-making is _____ and that in

this day and age, we don't _____.

Part 4

12. In Olivier Marc's quote, "crossed the threshold and shut the door behind us,"

does not necessarily refer to _____ or _____.

13. A currency trader in New York has video monitors all around his

apartment so he can _____.

14. More Americans will face the issues of blurred boundaries of work

and home as computers and gadgets become _____ and

_____.

15. _____ around the country felt that their home was not a refuge.

C. LISTENING AND MAKING INFERENCES

Listen to the excerpts from the interview and circle the best answers. Compare your answers with those of other students.

1. How does reporter Liane Hansen's personal experience illustrate the theme of blurred boundaries between work and home?
   a. Her daughter moved out of her mother's home to a studio apartment.
   b. The interview with Maggie Jackson was conducted in her home.
   c. Her engineer came to her home to help her conduct an interview with Jackson in New York.

2. How often do you think Jackson hurried her kids to bed so she could get back to work?
   a. only once
   b. several times
   c. every night

3. What does Hansen think about the boundaries of her new home office?
   a. They can be set physically.
   b. They can be set psychologically.
   c. They can be set both physically and psychologically.

4. What does the Olivier Marc quote mean?
   a. The architecture of the home is still important.
   b. Home is a place of comfort and protection.
   c. We are in danger of our work and home life becoming blurred.

A. USAGE: EXPRESSIONS OF CONTRAST

Notice   Listen to the following excerpts from the interview. What is the purpose of the boldfaced phrases in these statements? Are these ideas the main ideas of the speaker?

Excerpt 1

The fusion of work and home is not a new phenomenon. In earlier centuries, many families lived above the store, but Maggie Jackson says that **while there are similarities**, there are also major differences.

Excerpt 2

Liane Hansen: You wrote about, for example, trying to hurry your kids to bed so you could get back to work.

Maggie Jackson: Yes, that was—**although I can't say it only happened just once**—that was a sort of eureka moment.

Explanation   The boldfaced parts of the excerpts above are examples of **adverbial clauses of contrast**. They are used to indicate a contrasting idea to the main idea of the sentence. For example, as shown in the first excerpt, Jackson believes that there are similarities between earlier centuries and today in terms of the fusion of work and home, but she is more concerned with the differences. Likewise, in the second example, she is more interested in focusing on the fact that she hurried her kids off to bed in order to get back to work (and had a eureka moment) than the fact that she can't say it only happened once.

Adverbial clauses of contrast can be written before or after the main idea. For example, Jackson's idea could also be written as:

> *I hurried my kids off to bed so I could get back to work,* ***although I can't say it only happened just once***.

The following words and phrases can be used to introduce adverbial clauses of contrast:

although
though
even though
while[1]
despite the fact that
in spite of the fact that

---

[1]*while:* Use this conjunction to introduce the adverbial clause of contrast at the beginning of the sentence.

Exercise

Combine the statements into one sentence, using the word or phrase in parentheses. Consider the ideas expressed in the interview to decide which sentence is the contrasting idea. Remember to use a comma between the clauses. The first one has been done for you.

1. Our minds are in a different place. Our bodies can be home because of technology. (though)

   Though our bodies can be home because of technology, our minds are

   in a different place.

2. People are losing the sense of home as a refuge. Technology is helping people create more flexible work situations. (while)

   _____

   _____

   _____

3. Maggie Jackson found she was hurrying her kids to bed so that she could get back to work. She could be home to eat dinner, put the kids to bed, and read them a story. (while)

   _____

   _____

   _____

4. Jackson had a lot of flexibility working at home. She found that her work was seeping, leaking, and bleeding into the rest of her house. (although)

   _____

   _____

   _____

5. Liane Hansen feels the presence of her office in her house. She loves sitting comfortably at home, drinking coffee, and enjoying the beautiful view. (despite the fact that)

   _____

   _____

   _____

6. Hansen can create a physical boundary by closing the door to her office. She wonders how to create psychological boundaries between work and home. (even though)

_____

_____

_____

7. Most people who experience the fusion of work and home are in high-tech, high-paying jobs. More people will be facing the issue as technology becomes less expensive. (in spite of the fact that)

_____

_____

_____

B. PRONUNCIATION: CONTRASTIVE STRESS

Notice **Listen to the excerpt. Which words are stressed? Why?**

Excerpt

The fusion of work and home is not a new phenomenon. In earlier centuries, many families lived above the store, but Maggie Jackson says that while there are similarities, there are also major differences.

Explanation In the example above, the reporter compares working at home now and in the past. She focuses on the similarities and differences. If we want to highlight these contrastive words, we place more stress on them. They are also pronounced at a higher pitch. The stress on these words signals to the listeners that two points are being contrasted.

Exercise

Work in pairs. Take turns reading the following statements of contrast. Read the statements with contrastive stress. Place more stress and use a higher pitch on the capitalized words. Change roles after item 5.

1. Working from home, Maggie Jackson had more FLEXIBILITY, but less FOCUS on her work.

2. She was with her family PHYSICALLY, but not with them PSYCHOLOGICALLY.

3. Your BODY is at home, but your MIND is elsewhere.

4. While working from home, she could LOOK at a beautiful view, but she could only THINK about work.

5. While she was GAINING technology, she was LOSING her family.

Change roles.

6. Jackson could interview people on the WEST coast while she was working late on the EAST coast.

7. The OFFICE might be far away, but the WORK is next door.

8. Not only HIGH-TECH workers but also LOW-TECH workers will find themselves working more from home.

9. Home allows us to create an area of PEACE, but it also forces us to create an area of COMPROMISE.

10. Secretaries might be on VACATION, but they're WORKING every day.

C. DISCOURSE ANALYSIS: REFERRING TO PRIOR DISCOURSE

Notice   Listen to the excerpt from the interview. What word does the interviewer, Liane Hansen, use that Maggie Jackson then repeats? How many times does Jackson use that word again in her answer? What do you think is the purpose of this type of repetition?

Excerpt

Hansen: How else can one set psychological boundaries in the home to keep work from interfering, aside from a physical boundary?

Jackson: Well, I think that "boundary" is the perfect word to use because I am certainly not saying that all technology automatically means that work takes over your life or that, in this day and age, all the changes that are going on are bad. I think that the—you know, we're making the boundaries more flexible, but boundary-making is important, and I think that in this age we don't make enough boundaries.

Explanation   In the excerpt, Jackson expresses agreement with Hansen's use of the word "boundary" by answering her question with that word. She says it's the perfect word and then uses it four times in her answer. This style of speaking helps move a conversation forward. By using each other's words, speakers share meaning or understanding in discourse. This is an effective tool in conversation.

Exercise

Work in pairs. Student A reads the statement, which introduces the boldfaced word or phrase. Student B responds to the statement, using the boldfaced word or phrase three or four times. Change roles after each item. The first one has been done for you.

1. **Student A:** If you work at home and rarely go into the office, don't you think there is a problem of **visibility**[2]?

   Student B: Well, yes, I do. **Visibility** is always an issue. Your colleagues rarely see you, so you're less important. I think people who work from home need to maintain their **visibility** at work by attending important meetings and checking into the office now and then. **Visibility** might also be improved with occasional meetings with colleagues on Skype.

2. **Student A:** Working at home doesn't mean cutting back on working hours. In fact, most people working from home tend to work more and have problems with **time management**.

   Student B: _____

3. **Student B:** The best part about working from home is that you spend less money on gas and less time commuting to work. It's so much more **economical**!

   Student A: _____

4. **Student A:** Everyone talks about the benefits of working from home, but it's not easy having your family and work in the same place. **Multitasking** is never really effective!

   Student B: _____

5. **Student B:** It's great to work from home. I can stay in my pajamas all day, work my own hours, and enjoy a feeling of **independence**.

   Student A: _____

6. **Student A:** I think that when you don't work in the office, people always suspect that you're not doing your job. There's an issue of **trust**.

   Student B: _____

7. **Student B:** Since everybody brings their work home with them these days, home is no longer the **refuge** it used to be.

   Student A: _____

---

[2]*visibility:* being seen face-to-face by your coworkers on a regular basis

A. DISCUSSION QUESTIONS

Work in groups. Discuss your answers to the questions.

1. How can psychological boundaries be set so that the lines between work and home do not become too blurred? Can you offer any suggestions?

2. Discuss the meaning of the following titles and excerpts from poems and songs, and how they might or might not relate to the fusion of work and home in today's world.

> *You Can't Go Home Again.*
> — title of a 1940 novel by Thomas Wolfe

> Good-bye, proud world! I'm going home;
> Thou art not my friend and I'm not thine.
> — excerpt from poem by Ralph Waldo Emerson

> Keep the home fires burning,
> While your hearts are yearning;
> Though your lads are far away
> They dream of home.
> There's a silver lining
> Through the dark cloud shining;
> Turn the dark cloud inside out,
> Till the boys come home.
> — excerpt from 1914 song by Lena Guilbert Ford

> Mid pleasures and palaces though we may roam,
> Be it ever so humble, there's no place like home.
> — excerpt from 1823 song by John Howard Payne

> How does it feel
> To be on your own
> With no direction home
> Like a complete unknown
> Like a rolling stone?
> — excerpt from 1965 song by Bob Dylan

> Home is the place where
> when you have to go there,
> they have to take you in.
> — Excerpt from 1914 poem by Robert Frost

B. INTERVIEW: WORKING AT HOME

1. Take Notes to Prepare

Focusing on Liane Hansen's and Maggie Jackson's experiences and observations will help you recognize some of the advantages and disadvantages of fusing work and home, and prepare you for the interview that follows.

Listen to the interview again. Take notes on the issues involved with the fusing of office and home. Main topics and some examples have been provided for you.

Changes observed when work and home are fused:

a bedroom turns into a mini-studio

_____

_____

_____

Advantages of the work / home fusion:

more flexibility

_____

_____

_____

Disadvantages of the work / home fusion:

_____

_____

_____

_____

2. Write Interview Questions

Work in pairs. Write six to eight interview questions to ask someone who works at home. Try to find out how working at home has affected this person's life. Use the topics on page 58 to help you prepare your questions. Decide who you will interview.

3. Conduct Your Interview

One partner asks the interview questions, and the other takes notes.

Type of work done at home: _____

_____

_____

Length of time person has worked at home: _____

_____

_____

Changes at home as a result of working from home: _____

_____

_____

Changes in relationships with others: _____

_____

_____

Advantages of working at home: _____

_____

_____

Disadvantages of working at home: _____

_____

4. Oral Presentation

1. After you conduct your interview, plan an oral presentation with your partner. Divide your presentation so each of you has a chance to speak. Explain the advantages and disadvantages of working at home based on your interviewee's experience.

2. Follow the points in the box below. Your teacher or classmates may want to rate your presentation according to content interest, organization, pronunciation, fluency, grammar, and vocabulary.

Useful Points for Oral Presentations

When you make an oral presentation, consider the following:

1. Present a brief outline of your talk in the introduction. Give the audience a general overview of your talk.

2. Provide handouts for the audience.

3. Ask rhetorical questions, i.e., questions that engage the audience's listening but are not to be answered (For example, "Can you imagine what her home office looks like?").

4. Look at the audience. Check your notes but always look at the audience when you speak.

"What's Happening to Home?" was first broadcast on All Things Considered, *March 21, 2002. The interviewer is Liane Hansen.*

UNIT 5

Is Autism Underestimated?

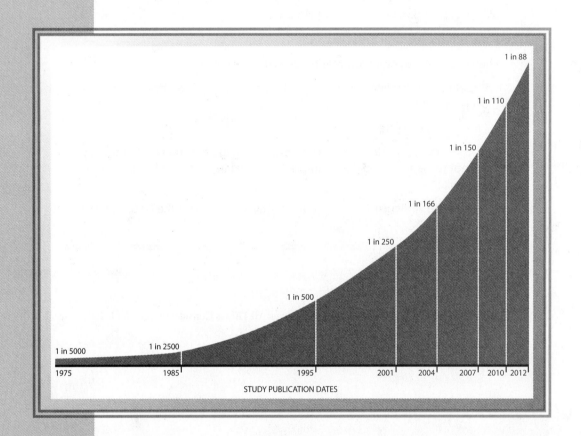

1 in 88

1 in 110

1 in 150

1 in 166

1 in 250

1 in 500

1 in 5000

1 in 2500

1975   1985   1995   2001   2004   2007 2010 2012

STUDY PUBLICATION DATES

I.   ANTICIPATING THE ISSUE

Discuss your answers to the questions.

1. From the title and information shown in the graph, what do you think the report in this unit is about?

2. What do you know about autism? How common is it in your country?

3. Why do you think autism is on the rise?

Read the text. Use the context to help you understand the meaning of the boldfaced words. Write the number of each word or phrase next to its meaning at the end of the text.

Autism is a brain **(1) disorder** that affects more and more people in the world each year. More boys than girls have the disorder. Though not well understood, autism seems to have a strong genetic basis; yet, it is complex, and some say it may be related to toxic materials in the environment. Autism affects the way information is processed in the brain, but it may also cause serious physical illnesses. Autism is one of three disorders on the **(2) spectrum** of autism disorders, the other two being Asperger Syndrome and Pervasive Developmental Disorder–Not Otherwise Specified (PDD-NOS).

A child with autism usually shows signs of autistic behavior by the age of three. Some **(3) telltale** behavioral signs of autism are: repetitive behaviors, such as head nodding or rocking the body back and forth; avoidance of eye contact; difficulty making friends or developing social relationships with **(4) peers**; resistance to change; and **(5) awkward** physical movements. If parents notice these signs in their child, they usually request to have their child **(6) screened** for autism. The screening involves an observation of the child's behavior. If the child shows at least six symptoms from a list of behaviors related to social interaction, communication, and physical movement, he or she may be **(7) diagnosed** as autistic.

(8) Tracking autism cases worldwide has been difficult. The disorder is not recognized in all countries. This is largely because autism continues to carry a **(9) stigma** in many parts of the world; families do not always want to admit that their child might have a mental disorder. However, in recent years, with new research providing a clearer understanding of the disorder, more and more cases of autism have been identified. In fact, the **(10) prevalence** of autism spectrum disorders has dramatically increased over the last few decades. The current estimate is that it affects more than 1 percent of American children.

When parents learn that their child has been diagnosed with autism, they often feel **(11) devastated**, realizing that such a diagnosis will have serious **(12) implications** for their child's future. They wonder whether their child will be able to study in a **(13) mainstream** school environment, or whether a specialized classroom will be necessary. They wonder whether their child will be able to live and work independently as an adult. Raising an autistic child can be very stressful for families; thus, support groups have been created to help families cope with autism.

_____ a. results; consequences

_____ b. normal, typical, general

_____ c. entire range

_____ d. an abnormal health condition

_____ e. closely following

_____ f. people of same age, status

_____ g. observed and evaluated

_____ h. destroyed; ruined

_____ i. clumsy; unskillful

_____ j. informative; revealing

_____ k. cause of shame or embarrassment

_____ l. how often something occurs

_____ m. identified medically by signs or symptoms

A. LISTENING FOR MAIN IDEAS

Listen to the report. After each of the five parts, you will hear a beep. Write the main idea in a complete sentence, using the key word or phrase given. Then compare your sentences with those of another student.

Part 1   autism study

_____

_____

Part 2   prevalence

_____

_____

Part 3   surprise

_____

_____

Part 4   children missed

_____

_____

Part 5   shouldn't be surprised

_____

_____

Read the questions for Part 1. Then listen to Part 1 again and circle the best answers. Compare your answers with those of another student. If your answers are different, listen again.

1. Why is the number of children diagnosed with autism going up?
   a. Autism is becoming more common.
   b. People are better at identifying it.
   c. The reason is not clear.

2. What is true about the study?
   a. Children were selected for the study.
   b. A single community was studied.
   c. The number of autism cases was expected.

Repeat the same procedure for Parts 2–5.

Part 2

3. To identify children with autism, most studies look at kids who . . .
   a. don't have an education.
   b. have special language skills.
   c. are having problems in school.

4. What location did the group choose for their study?
   a. small-sized city
   b. a city similar to one in the United States
   c. a city in South Korea, near Seoul

5. What percentage of children was found to be autistic?
   a. 55 percent
   b. 7 to 12 percent
   c. 2.64 percent

6. What percentage of the children with autism was in mainstream schools?
   a. half
   b. a third
   c. two-thirds

7. What is true about the children they identified?
   a. Many were in mainstream schools.
   b. They had already been recognized.
   c. They were already being treated for autism.

8. What do the researchers believe about the results of their study?
   a. Something is different about South Korean children.
   b. Autism is more common than people think.
   c. Only 38 kids in South Korea are affected by autism.

9. What expectation did Young-Shin Kim have?
   a. that the results would be a bit higher
   b. that children from the general population would not affect their study
   c. that the extent of their study would be greater

Part 4

10. Why were so many autistic children NOT identified?
    a. because they were misbehaving and failing academically
    b. because they were meeting expectations
    c. because they were having difficulties with their peers

11. Why else might autism not be identified in South Korea?
    a. because it carries a severe stigma
    b. because parents cannot recognize telltale behaviors
    c. because people are too upset to help their kids

12. How did some parents react when they learned their kids had autism?
    a. They didn't respond.
    b. They couldn't make sense of the information.
    c. They were happy to know what it was.

Part 5

13. What do we know about brain disorders?
    a. They are more common than autism.
    b. Depression and anxiety are common.
    c. They occur in 7 percent of the population.

14. Which of the following is typical among kids with autism?
    a. They have no friends.
    b. They get into trouble.
    c. They look odd.

C. LISTENING AND MAKING INFERENCES

Listen to the excerpts from the interview and circle the best answers. Compare your answers with those of other students.

1. What attitude does Professor Roy Richard Grinker express with this data?
   a. He thinks the results are very surprising.
   b. He isn't sure the results are correct.
   c. The results are what he expected.

2. How surprised does Young-Shin Kim seem to be with the results of their study?
   a. extremely
   b. somewhat
   c. not at all

3. Why does Professor Bennett Leventhal ask and then answer this question?
   a. He is not sure about his answer.
   b. He thinks people might not believe him.
   c. He wants to show that more research needs to be done.

IV. LOOKING AT LANGUAGE

A. USAGE: NEGATIVE PREFIXES

Notice A prefix is a letter or groups of letters that partly indicate the meaning of a word. Listen to the following excerpts. Notice the words with prefixes that form negative meaning. The prefixes have been underlined.

Excerpt 1

Two-thirds of the children with autism that we ended up identifying were in mainstream schools—<u>un</u>recognized, <u>un</u>treated.

Excerpt 2

I had some expectation that it's going to be a little higher than the previous studies because we're including children from the general population that were <u>under</u>studied in the past.

Excerpt 3

Kim says many of the children were probably missed because they didn't <u>mis</u>behave, and they weren't failing academically.

Excerpt 4

After all, brain <u>dis</u>orders, like depression and anxiety, occur in several percent of the population as well.

Explanation   There are a number of prefixes in English that form the negative or opposite meaning of a word. Here are some examples with adjectives:

Negative prefix	Examples
a-	atypical, apolitical
anti-	antisocial, antitraditional
dis-	dishonest, disrespectful
il-	illogical, illiterate
im-	impolite, impatient
in-	incomprehensible, inappropriate
ir-	irregular, irresponsible
mal-	maladjusted, malformed
mis-	misunderstood, misrepresented
over-	overdone, overprescribed
non-	nonverbal, noncompliant
un-	uncommon, unfocused
under-	understudied, underestimated

Exercise

Work in groups. Read the sentences. Fill in the blanks with the appropriate negative prefix from the list above. Use a dictionary if necessary.

1. For many years, autism was one of the most _____ diagnosed disorders affecting children. The term "mental retardation" was used instead.

2. Our knowledge of the causes of autism is _____ sufficient

    and _____ complete.

3. Scientists have found that the brain function of an autistic child is

    _____ regular.

4. It is probably _____ possible to design one treatment program that meets the needs of all autistic children.

5. The behavior of autistic children is often considered

    _____ typical. They may exhibit repetitive behaviors or focus on small details.

6. In American school systems, it is _____ legal to discriminate against autistic children. They have the right to equal educational opportunities.

7. Autistic children typically exhibit _____ social behaviors. They may have trouble making friends and connecting with peers.

8. The needs of siblings of autistic children are often

_____recognized. These children do not always receive the attention they need from their parents.

9. Some families do not report autism because government support is

_____existent; society has a stigma toward the disorder.

10. Scientists believe that some of the neurological pathways of an autistic

person's brain are _____connected.

11. Adults with autism are _____represented. The media tends to focus only on children suffering from the disorder.

12. An autistic child may be _____adjusted to meet the needs of the mainstream classroom.

13. The fact that autistic children can be taught the life skills they need to

work in jobs may be _____emphasized. Many autistic adults actually need supervision in places of work.

B. PRONUNCIATION: STRESS CHANGES WITH PREFIXES

Notice Listen to the following excerpts. Pay attention to the words with negative prefixes. Notice the stressed syllable (the syllable that is pronounced more strongly) in each boldfaced word.

Excerpt 1

Two-thirds of the children with autism that we ended up identifying were in mainstream schools—**unREcognized, unTREAted.**

Excerpt 2

I had some expectation that it's going to be a little higher than the previous studies because we're including children from the general population that were **underSTUdied** in the past.

Excerpt 3

Kim says many of the children were probably missed because they didn't **misbeHAVE** and they weren't failing academically.

Excerpt 4

After all, brain **disORders** like depression and anxiety occur in several percent of the population as well.

Explanation When prefixes are added to root words, the general stress pattern does not usually change. The prefix has secondary, or weaker, stress. The root of the word maintains its primary, or stronger, stress.

Some prefixes, such as *under-*, *over-*, and *up-*, are prepositions. When added to a verb, these prefixes can form nouns and adjectives, for example, in the word *understudied*. When prepositional prefixes form adjectives, the stress is on the root of the word, as in *overloaded*. However, when prepositional prefixes form nouns, the pattern tends to be reversed: The stress is on the prepositional prefix, as in *overload*.

Exercise 1

Work in pairs. Read the sentences and decide whether the boldfaced words are nouns or adjectives. On the line, write *N* (noun) or *A* (adjective). Then underline the stressed syllable in each word.

_____ 1. There has been a **downturn** in the practice of isolating children who are different.

_____ 2. The need for care for adults with autism in the future is **underestimated**.

_____ 3. Kids with autism feel like **outcasts** when they are among their peers.

_____ 4. Some people believe that the rise in autism cases comes from our **overdose** of toxic chemicals every day.

_____ 5. The data on autism around the world is **incomplete**.

_____ 6. A **byproduct** of caring for kids with autism may be the discovery of our capacity to love.

_____ 7. Autistic children may become nervous or upset when they are **overexposed** to noise and activity.

_____ 8. Children with diseases such as cancer are now **outnumbered** by the number of children with autism.

_____ 9. Teachers need more **input** from psychologists in how to teach kids with autism.

_____ 10. A common **offshoot** for kids with autism is a set of unusual talents and abilities.

Exercise 2

Work in pairs. Take turns reading the sentences in Exercise 1 aloud. Be sure to use the correct stress. Look up at your partner when you speak.

C. DISCOURSE ANALYSIS: DISCOURSE MARKERS

Notice   Listen to the excerpt from the report. Notice the boldfaced words in the statements. What do they mean here?

Excerpt

Some of the parents were yelling at us, **like**, "You guys are crazy. My child is OK," and getting really angry about it. Some of the parents were shocked. Some are devastated. But some are **like**, "Oh, my God, now it makes sense."

Explanation   The word **like** in English can be used for many different purposes. *Like* can be used as the following:

1. a preposition: used in similes (to compare two dissimilar ideas)

   *His eyes are **like** stones. He doesn't seem to see me.*

2. a subordinating conjunction in place of *as* or *as if*

   *That child acts **like** he's on the spectrum.*

   *(That child acts **as** / **as if** he's on the spectrum.)*

3. a verb: referring to a fondness for someone or something

   *Joshua **likes** his teacher and has formed a bond with her.*

4. an interjection in colloquial speech / slang (This usage is very common among young, native-English speakers; it replaces *um, uh, you know.*)

   *He, **like**, never says anything!*

5. an adverb: meaning "nearly" or to indicate exaggeration

   *He was, **like**, ready to kill me.*

6. a hedge: an informal phrase to indicate approximation

   *The school is **like two** minutes from here.*

7. an introduction to quoted speech (replacing *say* or *think*)

   *She was **like**, "Leave me alone for awhile."*

In the excerpt from Young-Shin Kim above, the usage of **like** is to introduce quoted speech, as in example 7. By using **like** in place of *saying*, Kim may be introducing the parents' speech without using their exact words, but by giving an approximate quote. In this way, the use of **like** is also a hedge, as in example 6.

Experts on public speaking often recommend that speakers avoid overuse of discourse markers and fillers, such as *like, um, uh,* and *you know.* Using too many of these discourse markers throughout a presentation can make a speaker sound less confident. The audience may believe that the speaker does not have a clear understanding of what he or she is talking about.

Exercise 1

Listen to the mini-dialogues. Which speaker sounds more confident? Circle *male* or *female*. Compare your answers with those of another student. Discuss the differences between the two speakers and their use of discourse markers. Listen again if necessary.

1. male female
2. male female
3. male female
4. male female

Exercise 2

Work in pairs. Take turns giving one-minute talks on the following topics. Each student gives two talks. Do <u>not</u> prepare your ideas before speaking. While one student speaks, the other counts the number of discourse markers used. When the speaker finishes, comment on how discourse markers affected your impressions of the talk.

- The increasing prevalence of autism
- The causes of autism
- The stigma associated with having an autistic child
- Autistic children in mainstream classrooms

V. FOLLOW-UP ACTIVITIES

A. DISCUSSION QUESTIONS

Work in groups. Discuss your answers to the questions.

1. Why might there be such a stigma associated with autism? What other medical conditions present a stigma to society? What can be done about this problem?

2. In a TV series on autism, Dr. Gerald Fishbach describes his research on autism by saying:

   > "I think we're addressing one of the most profound problems in not only all of medicine but in all of human existence. We're talking about the ability to relate to other people, to empathize in a certain way and to comprehend. And I think it's the most worthwhile, most challenging effort in science that I've ever been involved in."

   Do you agree that autism is one of the most profound problems in human existence?

B. CASE STUDY: MICKEY TEUBERT

1. Take Notes to Prepare

Taking notes on some of the questions and assumptions about autism in the report will help you evaluate the case study that follows.

Listen to the report again. Take notes on key points regarding the study conducted in South Korea. Key phrases and examples have been provided for you. Use your notes to help you discuss the case study that follows.

Number of children with autism going up:

- _____

- _____

Most efforts to identify autism:

- *kids in special education classes* _____

- _____

- _____

Findings in South Korean study:

- *prevalence of 2.64%* _____

- _____

- _____

- _____

- _____

Reasons children were missed:

- *didn't misbehave* _____

- _____

- _____

- *autism stigma in South Korea—parents ignored it?* ___

Reactions of parents learning their kid is "on the spectrum":

- *upset, yelling, angry* _____
- _____
- _____

Issues for kids with autism:

- *socially awkward* _____
- _____

Teach them skills:

- _____

2. Consider the Issue

You have listened to issues related to a study of autism conducted in South Korea. In the case below, the parents of an autistic child, Mickey Teubert, must confront the issue of whether or not their child should attend a mainstream school.

Read the case.

Mickey Teubert was adopted at the age of two. After having completed the necessary steps for an international adoption, his parents flew to his orphanage in Russia and brought him home to live with his new American family. But when Mickey was four years old, his parents began to notice that their son had some developmental problems: He did not seem to be progressing at the same rate as his peers. Knowing that kids who are adopted from orphanages often need time to catch up, they did not worry too much. But by the age of five, they realized that Mickey had some of the telltale signs of autism: He was talking to himself, playing alone, and not showing much interest in other people. They decided that he should be tested; the diagnosis showed that Mickey was on the autism spectrum. Mickey's parents were devastated. At the time, there were no special classes designed for children with autism; these children were simply placed in mainstream classes with special accommodations.

By the time Mickey reached fourth grade, the elementary school had created a special-needs classroom for children with autism, so Mickey was able to finish elementary school in special classes, with some participation in the regular classes and programs. But when he was ready to move into middle school, a decision had to be made about where and how he should continue his studies. Should he remain *excluded* in the "autism classroom," to be educated only with peers with autism but receive the one-on-one attention of an aide? Or should he be *included* in regular classes, where he would interact with typical kids but work with teachers who were not trained in special education?

The middle school was willing to include Mickey with typical kids in certain classes and school settings, such as art class, music class, and the lunchroom. But his mom wanted him included in some of the academic classes as well. She was convinced that her son could succeed in a class like science, a fairly concrete subject. If his science program could be modified, and if he could be prepared for his regular classes during his special-needs class time, she felt he could attain a higher level of achievement and stronger sense of self-esteem. She had to fight to get her son placed in regular academic classes, but the school finally allowed Mickey into the regular science class, albeit for only 20 of the 50 minutes of the regularly scheduled class.

More recently, Mickey took a cooking class with typical kids. The kids were asked to help direct Mickey in the kitchen to make sure he did his share of the work, but the kids did not always want to take on this responsibility; they were more interested in completing their own work or didn't feel comfortable taking on a supervisory role. But in a different extracurricular experience, Mickey was paired with a typical boy in a theater production class, and at the end of that class, the boy told his mother that he felt he had learned more from Mickey than Mickey had learned from him. The opportunity for typical kids to benefit from shared learning experiences with kids with autism is undeniable. It opens them up to communication with students who are challenged by learning and emotional differences.

Has education been successful for Mickey? This is not clear. Because an autistic child will not come home and report on his successes or failures at school, parents do not always hear from the child himself about how things are going. In fact, Mickey has never expressed pride or disappointment about his work. His mom is not sure that Mickey even notices the difference between the mainstream or special-needs classrooms. She also admits that if Mickey is not at the same cognitive level of his peers in academic subjects, there may be no advantage to his joining them.

From another perspective, not all parents of typical kids are happy to have their children in a class with special-needs students. They are afraid that a child with autism can disrupt their kids' education, since that child requires much more attention from the teacher. They also point out that the cost of supplying an aide, as well as other special accommodations, for the child with autism in a regular classroom can cost as much as 1.6 times the cost of a general education.

3. Role-play

Break the class into three groups. Assign each group one of the following roles:

> Mickey's parents
> School teachers
> Parents of other children in the school

Consider the opinions and views of your group's assigned role. Discuss the pros and cons of including Mickey, a child with autism, in mainstream classes. List concerns and recommendations for your role.

ROLE	
PROS	
CONS	
CONCERNS / RECOMMENDATIONS	

Meet as a class. Present your group's arguments and recommendations about whether or not to include Mickey in a mainstream school. Try to reach a decision about Mickey's schooling.

"Is Autism Underestimated?" was first broadcast on Morning Edition *May 9, 2011. The reporter is Jon Hamilton.*

Medicine by the Minute

I. ANTICIPATING THE ISSUE

Discuss your answers to the questions.

1. From the title and the picture, discuss what you think the report in this unit is about.

2. If you have to visit the doctor in your country, who pays, you or your health insurance? Describe how the system works.

3. What kinds of things do you typically visit the doctor for? At the office, how long do you have to wait before you see a doctor? How long does the doctor usually spend with you? What kinds of services do you expect when you visit a doctor?

4. Describe the health care system where you live. Are people generally happy or unhappy with the services?

Read the text. Use the context to help you understand the meaning of the boldfaced words and phrases. Write the number of each word or phrase next to its meaning at the end of the text.

When most Americans go to the doctor, the first question they are usually asked is not what's wrong with them but what kind of insurance they have. In most cases, patients are now asked to pay their (**1**) **co-pay** even before seeing the doctor. Doctors want to be sure that the patient will pay his or her share of medical costs before they request the insurance payment. In today's world, doctors, medical office workers, and patients are consumed by the administration of managed care, a system of health care that has become very common in the United States. Under this system, patients have insurance that allows them to use only particular doctors or hospitals, and that sometimes limits the kinds of medicine, tests, or procedures that they can get.

In the managed care system, doctors have to fill out a lot of insurance forms and follow many rules in order for insurance companies to pay them for a patient's treatment. Even if doctors follow the correct procedures, companies sometimes refuse to pay. With the added time required to argue with insurance companies so that patients' bills can be paid, (**2**) **primary care** doctors have been forced to cut back on patient care. Some doctors may now be required to see up to eight patients in an hour to make up for the time and money lost spent completing paperwork. Many no longer have any time to work "off the clock"[1] when patients might need special attention.

Many doctors and patients have "had it." They are (**3**) **fed up with** this system and would like to see a change. They think medicine doesn't work when business controls the medical world. In fact, some doctors are beginning to leave the system, even though they will make only half of their salary. For example, some doctors are opening up their own clinics in order to treat patients for (**4**) **acute care**. Instead of accepting insurance and dealing with all the administrative headaches, they give patients an (**5**) **itemized** bill and ask to be paid in cash at the end of each visit. So, like a car (**6**) **mechanic** who charges for labor and parts, an (**7**) **osteopath** or other doctor who sees a patient for a back injury might charge for his or her time and the individual medical supplies used in treatment.

These clinics offer some relief to patients, as well. Instead of spending days waiting to see their primary physician for a (**8**) **bruise** or cut, patients can now walk in and see a doctor in 10-15 minutes, and they can have more immediate and personal contact with a doctor. Often, the price a patient pays for this service is not much higher than an insurance co-pay. The patient may have to pay for the (**9**) **suture tray** because the doctor's instruments need to be (**10**) **sterilized** after use. He or she may have to pay for an (**11**) **injection** because the doctor has to (**12**) **anesthetize** the person. But in the end, the expenses are generally the same as the co-pay required by insurance companies.

Cash-only clinics may be the way of the future as people become more and more dissatisfied with the managed healthcare system.

---

[1] *off the clock:* overtime without pay

_____ a. main source of medical care provided by one's insurance company

_____ b. with individual items and services listed

_____ c. a doctor who treats muscles and bones

_____ d. a method of giving drugs or medication through a needle

_____ e. tray with material for sewing a wound

_____ f. someone who repairs motor vehicles and machinery

_____ g. medical care for people with injuries or illnesses that need help urgently

_____ h. give drugs to help stop pain

_____ i. fee paid by insured patients for doctor's visit

_____ j. purple or brown mark on your skin from a fall or hit

_____ k. completely cleaned from any bacteria

_____ l. tired of

III. LISTENING

A. LISTENING FOR MAIN IDEAS

Listen to the interview. After each of the five parts, you will hear a beep. Write the main idea in a complete sentence, using the key word or phrase given. Then compare your sentences with those of another student. The first one has been done for you.

Part 1 clinic

Dr. Lisa Grigg opened a medical clinic in Vermont that accepts no

insurance.

Part 2 charge

_____

_____

Part 3 simple

_____

_____

Part 4 ▶ acute care

_____

_____

Part 5 ▶ stop the clock

_____

_____

B. LISTENING FOR DETAILS

Read the sentences for Part 1. Listen to Part 1 again and fill in the blanks with the missing information. Compare your answers with those of another student. If your answers are different, listen again.

Part 1 ▶

1. Dr. Lisa Grigg "had it" with insurance _____ and insurance

   _____.

2. She hung out a shingle[2] as a(n) _____ provider.

3. Patients are charged according to a(n) _____ schedule that they can easily understand.

Repeat the same procedure for Parts 2–5.

Part 2 ▶

4. Grigg charges _____ a minute for labor.

5. In addition to charging for her labor when treating a bruise or cut, Dr.

   Grigg would also have to charge for a(n) _____ and a(n)

   _____.

6. Her itemized bill would show the charge by the _____ and

   by the _____.

_____

[2]*shingle:* opened a new business

7. Grigg was feeling _____ managed care.

8. With managed care, she felt that there was an awful lot of

   _____, an awful lot of tail chasing, and an awful lot of

   _____ with insurances for tests or medicines.

9. Like at her mechanic's, Grigg has a(n) _____ hanging up in her office.

10. Average co-pays are between _____ and

    _____ dollars.

11. Grigg encourages people to stay with their _____ physicians.

12. At her last job, Grigg spent about _____ hours a day with

    patients and _____ to _____ hours a day making phone calls or doing paperwork.

13. Interviewer Robert Siegel wonders if Grigg has a blanket rule[3] for

    _____, no matter what the problem is.

14. Grigg's office manager feels that Lisa should be _____

    _____ more.

15. If Grigg thinks a(n) _____ is something more serious, then she will sit and talk with a patient.

16. Siegel thinks Grigg's _____ must be frustrated with their interview.

---

[3]*blanket rule:* general policy

C. LISTENING AND MAKING INFERENCES

Listen to the excerpts from the interview. Pay attention to each speaker's tone of voice and choice of words. What is their attitude? Circle the best answer for each question. Compare your answers with those of another student.

1. What attitude does Dr. Lisa Grigg express in her answers?
   a. humor
   b. embarrassment
   c. confidence

2. What attitude does interviewer Robert Siegel express in his comment to Grigg?
   a. surprise
   b. disbelief
   c. disappointment

3. What attitude does Grigg express toward phone calls and paperwork?
   a. acceptance
   b. annoyance
   c. anger

4. What attitude does Siegel express in his question?
   a. criticism
   b. disbelief
   c. humor

IV. LOOKING AT LANGUAGE

A. USAGE: PRESENT UNREAL VS. FUTURE REAL CONDITIONAL

Notice In the following excerpt, the interviewer, Robert Siegel, imagines that he is a patient who goes to Dr. Lisa Grigg's clinic for care. He presents his scenario as an unreal, imaginary case by using a condition clause with the term *Let's say,* which has the same meaning as *Imagine that . . .* or *If . . .* During the interview, however, the scenario starts to sound like a real case. Can you tell where this happens in the conversation? How does this change the structure of Siegel's later statements?

Excerpt

Robert Siegel:	Let's say I went in with, you know, a bruise or a cut and you had to bandage me up.
Dr. Lisa Grigg:	I'd still charge for my labor. I'd have to also charge for a suture tray because my instruments will have to be sterilized after I use them on you. And a little bit for an injection.
Siegel:	Hmm.
Grigg:	Hoping we want to anesthetize you.
Siegel:	So, I really get an itemized bill here, and I know exactly what I'm paying for.
Grigg:	Right.
Siegel:	And charge me by the minute and by the part.
Grigg:	Yep.

Explanation

In the excerpt above, Siegel presents a situation in which he would go to Grigg's clinic with a bruise or cut. He sees this as an imaginary, unreal situation.

The present unreal condition is formed as follows:

Condition clause (*if* clause)	Result clause
If + subject + past tense	subject + *would* + base verb
If Robert went *to the clinic and* ***had*** *to be bandaged up,*	***Dr. Grigg would charge*** *him for her labor.*

However, in the middle of the conversation, Grigg continues as if the situation were real. From that point on, the conversation continues in the future real conditional. This switch between unreal and real conditions sometimes occurs in everyday conversations.

The future real conditional is formed as follows:

Condition clause (*if* clause)	Result clause
If + subject + present tense	subject + *will* + base form
If I use *a suture tray,*	*my* ***instruments will have to be*** *sterilized after I use them.*

NOTE: The conditional clause can come *before* or *after* the result clause. The example above could also be expressed, "My instruments will have to be sterilized after I use them if I use a suture tray."

Exercise

Complete the sentences with information from the interview. Use the future real or present unreal conditionals of the verbs in parentheses.

1. If a patient comes to Grigg with a bruise or a cut, she _____ (charge) for labor, a suture tray, and an injection.

2. If Robert Siegel _____ (go) to Grigg's clinic, he would be charged by the minute and by the part.

3. If Grigg had more paperwork in her clinic, she _____ (not / spend) as much time as she does with her patients.

4. If Grigg _____ (accept) co-pays, she would have more paperwork.

5. Grigg _____ (tell) her patients to see their primary care physicians if they need more than acute care.

6. Grigg would go off-the-clock if she _____ (feel) a patient had a serious problem.

7. If Grigg gives a lot of off-the-clock time to her patients, her office manager _____ (get) frustrated with her.

B. PRONUNCIATION: /ʊ/ SOUND IN *WOULD*

Notice Listen to the excerpt from the interview. Focus on the boldfaced word in each result clause. How is it pronounced?

Excerpt

Robert Siegel: And if I visited your clinic, your office, **would** I see the price list up in the office?

Dr. Lisa Grigg: Yes, you **would**. It's a felt board with some pressed-in white letters and that's what it says on it: parts and labor.

Explanation The vowel sound in the word *would* is the same vowel sound as that in the common words *should* and *could*. To produce this vowel sound, do not round your lips. Drop your tongue toward the center of your mouth. This sound is sometimes hard for students as it does not exist in all languages. This is especially true when it follows the /w/ sound as in *would*.

A sound that is often confused with the /ʊ/ sound is /u/. Unlike the production of /ʊ/, /u/ is pronounced with the lips rounded to produce a glide ending with the sound /w/.

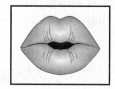

Exercise 1

Listen to each pair of words. Then work with a partner and practice pronouncing the contrasting vowel sounds in the two words.

1. would/wooed
2. should/shoed
3. could/cooed
4. stood/stewed
5. soot/suit
6. full/fool
7. pull/pool
8. hood/who'd
9. look/Luke
10. cook/kook

Exercise 2

Match the two parts of the mini-dialogues. Think about the pronunciation of each boldfaced word. Then listen to the dialogues to check your answers. Finally, work with a partner and read the dialogues aloud. Focus on the /ʊ/ and /u/ sounds.

Student A	Student B
_____ 1. **Luke**, you have a **bruise** on your leg!	a. I have a **good** diet **book** you **could** read.
_____ 2. My neck is **too** sore to **move**.	b. You **should** eat lighter meals, more vegetables and **fruit**.
_____ 3. Doctor, I **pulled** a muscle in my left leg again.	c. Come in at **noon**, and he can have a **look**.
_____ 4. I don't feel very **good** after that rich **food**.	d. You may be allergic to **wool**.
_____ 5. I need to **lose** 10 pounds to **look good** in that dress.	e. No, it's just **soot** from cleaning my fireplace today.
_____ 6. That **woman** has a terrible backache after bike riding all day.	f. You **shouldn't** have **stood** on it.
	g. OK, but **who** do you go to? You only just **moved** here.
_____ 7. Can you drive me to a doctor? I **cut** my **foot** pretty badly.	h. It **could** be that you spent too much time swimming in that **pool**!
_____ 8. Can the dentist see me today? I have a **loose tooth**.	i. She **could** get a massage to **soothe** it.
_____ 9. Doctor, why **would** I feel **super** itchy when I wear this sweater?	

C. DISCOURSE ANALYSIS: SHIFTS IN FOOTING

Notice Listen to the following excerpt from the interview. What different roles does the interviewer assume in this part of the conversation?

Excerpt

Dr. Lisa Grigg: I charge two dollars a minute for my labor, and we have to charge a little bit here and there for parts once in a while.

Robert Siegel: Let's say I went in with, you know, a bruise or a cut and you had to bandage me up.

Grigg:	I'd still charge for my labor. I'd have to also charge for a suture tray because my instruments will have to be sterilized after I use them on you, and a little bit for an injection.
Siegel:	Hmm.
Grigg:	Hoping we want to anesthetize you.

Explanation

Speakers often shift their "footing" during a conversation. In the excerpt above, Siegel moves from the role of reporter interviewing a doctor about her practice to the role of patient asking the doctor about his cut or bruise. We recognize this shift in footing by the reporter's change of voice. He adopts a different linguistic style, almost a different dialect. When he changes his voice, he also uses the first person, "I," and the doctor follows using "you" as if he is her patient. This type of role play of a real-life situation is common in everyday conversations. Speakers often "change hats" this way when they engage in dialogue.

Exercise 1

Read the dialogues. Underline the part of the conversation where there is a shift in footing. What new roles do the speakers take? Discuss your answers with the class.

Dialogue 1: *At an Employee Benefits Fair*

Employee:	Hi. I'm thinking of changing my health plan. Can you tell me about the plans you offer?
Insurance Agent:	Sure. We have several options described in our brochure. Please take a look.
Employee:	Is there a family policy with a low monthly payment?
Insurance Agent:	Look at this option.
Employee:	This looks good. Let's say I have to stay in the hospital, what does this plan cover?
Insurance Agent:	We cover 90 percent. But you need to pay a $150 co-pay if you are seen in the emergency room.
Employee:	And if I need to see a specialist?
Insurance Agent:	You pay the same amount. There's a $150 co-pay.

Dialogue 2: *At a Student Recruiting Fair*

Student:	Hello. I'm interested in finding out about nursing programs. I hear there is a shortage of nurses in hospitals.
Recruiting Officer:	Yes, you're right. Nurses are in high demand.
Student:	I don't want to invest a lot of time and money in going back to school.

Recruiting Officer:	Well, we have a nursing program that can be completed in just a year. I actually teach one of the courses in that program, Fundamentals of Nursing.
Student:	Hmm. OK. If I'm a student in your course, what would I study?
Recruiting Officer:	My course combines theory and practice. In my lab section, you learn how to prepare a suture tray, give injections, and monitor vital signs.
Student:	Do I practice on real patients?
Recruiting Officer:	No. That comes later in your nursing career.

Exercise 2

Work in pairs. On a separate piece of paper, write a dialogue in which the speakers change their footing during the conversation. Consider changes in discourse (voice, dialect, pronoun reference, etc.) as you prepare your dialogue. Then role-play the dialogue in class.

V. FOLLOW-UP ACTIVITIES

A. DISCUSSION QUESTIONS

Work in groups. Discuss your answers to the questions.

1. Would you go to Dr. Lisa Grigg's clinic for acute care? Why or why not? If so, in which circumstances would you go to her?

2. Grigg is an example of a person in one professional field borrowing ideas and systems from another field in order to become more effective. Can you think of other examples where this has been done? Share stories you know in which a professional used ideas or practices from a different profession to do a better job.

B. CASE STUDY: DIAL-A-DOC

1. Take Notes to Prepare

Focusing on Dr. Lisa Grigg's frustrations with the current systems in the medical field and the solutions she found will prepare you to evaluate the case study that follows.

Listen to the interview again. Take notes on Grigg's story. Main topics and some examples have been provided for you.

Fee schedule:

Patients charged according to a fee schedule they could understand

_____

_____

_____

_____

Types of patient care / needs:

acute care

_____

_____

_____

_____

Time with patients:

_____

_____

_____

_____

2. Consider the Issue

You have listened to how and why one doctor, Dr. Grigg, opened up her cash-only clinic. In the case described below, doctors equally frustrated with the managed care system found a very different solution to providing better patient care.

Read the case.

Many doctors and patients, frustrated with managed care and the lack of personal attention doctors are able to give patients these days, are seeking ways people can gain more control over their health. A few years ago, Brent Blue, a medical doctor from Wyoming, established "Dial-a-Doc," a service in which people can call up and speak to a doctor within 60 seconds. This is an attractive alternative to the time people usually spend trying to talk to their doctor, which involves scheduling an appointment, driving to the doctor's office, and sitting in the waiting room to see the doctor. Given the fact that 70 percent of doctors visits are made by people just looking for medical information, this service makes a lot of sense. Dial-a-Doc is available 24 hours a day, seven days a week and only costs about $2 a minute. The phone doctors are often retired doctors who want to continue working at home without having to travel to an office, attend meetings, or do paperwork. They work 12-hour shifts, evenly split between day and night. They can work a maximum of two shifts (24 hours) in a row.

Most of the calls doctors receive are from mothers who are anxious about their babies, people wondering if they really need to see a doctor, and people concerned about the medications they should or shouldn't be taking. Some people call Dial-a-Doc when they are afraid to ask their own doctor certain questions, or when they are looking for a second opinion.

Others use Dial-a-Doc for emergencies. Dial-a-Doc has received a significant amount of criticism. Although the service, and others like it, stresses that it neither diagnoses illness nor prescribes medication, callers often have the perception that they are getting medical care, and they will take any advice they get seriously. Yet, a phone call to a doctor is really just a conversation and not the same as an in-person interview or exam. The doctor and patient never meet. In addition, a research institute that studies consumer health information determined that over-the-phone medical advice is often incomplete and that doctors taking phone calls may be tempted to diagnose a problem rather quickly. Other critics point out that services such a Dial-a-Doc are a simple solution to a larger problem: They worry that, with such services, true healthcare reform may be further delayed.

As patients become more and more frustrated with managed care, this service is likely to become even more popular. Some predict that we may even be entering a new era of "information doctors," in which doctors will specialize in caring for people over the phone. Meanwhile, the American Medical Association is concerned about the usefulness and safety of such care. They are considering rules for call-in doctors.

3. Role-play

Work in a group. Imagine that you are members of a committee that is studying doctors' phone consultations. Make a list of problems that you see with Dial-a-Doc services. Then make a list of rules doctors must follow to prevent those problems. Compare your lists with those of the other groups.

PROBLEMS	RULES
Doctors don't see patients in person	Doctors can't diagnose illnesses or prescribe medicine.
Many Dial-a-Doc doctors are retired and may not know about the latest medical research	

"Medicine by the Minute" was first broadcast on All Things Considered *April 26, 2000. The interviewer is Robert Siegel.*

Tying the Knot

I.   ANTICIPATING THE ISSUE

Discuss your answers to the questions.

1. From the title and picture, what do you think the interview in this unit is about?

2. When do you think a person is ready to get married? What factors (for example, financial situation, children, etc.) do you think are important to consider before getting married?

3. In your country, how common is it for people to live together before they are married? How common is it for couples to have children without being married?

Exercise 1

Try to match the marriage facts in the left column to the countries in the right column. Compare your answers with those of your classmates. Then check your answers on page 103.

Marriage Facts

_____ 1. Approximately one-third of the men in rural areas "import" brides from other countries.

_____ 2. The average marrying age for men is over 30.

_____ 3. First and second cousins often marry.

_____ 4. This was the first country to legalize same-sex marriage.

_____ 5. More than half of children are born to couples living together but not married.

_____ 6. Young adults live with their parents until their 20s.

_____ 7. People marry more often, but they also divorce more often.

_____ 8. It is still common for parents to choose whom their children will marry.

_____ 9. Sixty percent of women are married before they are 18 years old.

_____ 10. A presidential candidate from this country had four children without ever marrying.

Countries

a. Spain and Italy

b. Sweden

c. South Korea

d. France

e. Nepal

f. India

g. The Netherlands

h. Saudi Arabia

i. The United States

j. Japan

Exercise 2

Read the mini-dialogues. Use the context to help you understand the meaning of the boldfaced words and phrases. Then circle the response that best fits the dialogue.

1. A: Almost half of U.S. marriages end in divorce. It seems that Europeans don't divorce as often as Americans do.

   B: Actually, according to the latest **census**, Swedes divorce almost as often as Americans.

   A: _____
      a. I find that data surprising.
      b. I don't understand it either.

2. A: Marriage has been on a sharp decline in recent years.

   B: Yes. I wonder what the **implications** are.

   A: _____
      a. I think it's because people are afraid of divorce.
      b. I think more people will live together without being married.

3. A: Why are you **postponing** your wedding? I thought you wanted to be married before you finished college.

   B: _____
      a. I love Matt, but I don't want to be married to him.
      b. I think we'll be in a better financial situation after college.

4. A: Were you nervous on your wedding day?

   B: I was fine until I was standing at the **altar**. Then I realized that my decision to stay with one person for the rest of my life was real!

   A: _____
      a. Yes. It's important to remember that marriage is more than just beautiful flowers and the wedding dress.
      b. I can't believe you're still thinking about your old boyfriend.

5. A: Sarah and David have been **partners** for years. I wonder if they will ever have children.

   B: _____
      a. I doubt it. They seem satisfied with just being a couple.
      b. Probably. That was their plan when they got married.

6. A: The divorce rate in the United States is **startling** to me. Almost half of marriages end in divorce.

   B: _____
      a. I agree. It's not surprising. The data never changes.
      b. You didn't know that? It's been that way for a while.

7. A: It's interesting that France has so many children born **out of wedlock**.

   B: _____
      a. That's because most people stay married for a long time.
      b. That's because 90 percent of young people choose to live together and not marry.

8. A: Why are so many people delaying marriage?

   B: I'm not sure, but I imagine the economy must **factor into** their decision.

   A: _____
      a. You're right. The cost of a wedding is incredible these days.
      b. You're right. Marriage doesn't have anything to do with money.

9. A: Weren't you and your boyfriend planning to get married this year?

   B: I think we'll probably wait another year because of the economic **recession**.

   A: _____
   a. Yeah, I'm sure it costs a lot of money to get married.
   b. Good idea. It takes a long time to plan a party.

10. A: Peter just asked Ashley to marry him!

    B: What are the **odds** that she'll say "yes"?

    A: _____
    a. I guess you're right. He is a little different.
    b. I think there's a pretty good chance.

11. A: In the last year, there was actually a **modest** decline in the divorce rate.

    B: Really, how much did it change?

    A: _____
    a. It dropped from 7.1 to 6.8 per 1,000 people.
    b. It dropped from 7.1 to 4.6 per 1,000 people.

12. A: It seems that no one believes in marriage anymore. Fewer and fewer people get married these days.

    B: That's why there are so many couples **cohabiting**.

    A: _____
    a. I guess most people prefer to stay single nowadays.
    b. Yes, but their legal benefits are unclear.

III. LISTENING

A. LISTENING FOR MAIN IDEAS

Listen to the interview. After each of the five parts, you will hear a beep. Write the main idea in your own words, using the key word or phrase given. Then compare your answers with those of another student.

Part 1   decline

_____

_____

Part 2   postponing marriage

_____

_____

Part 3   out of wedlock

_____

_____

Part 4   odds are huge

_____

_____

Part 5   cohabiting

_____

_____

B. LISTENING FOR DETAILS

Read the questions for Part 1. Then listen to Part 1 again and circle the best answer. Compare your answers with those of another student. If your answers are different, listen again.

Part 1

1. At what age do we see an especially sharp drop in marriage?
   a. from 25–34
   b. from 34–35
   c. from 35–46

2. How many young adults were married in 2000?
   a. 45 percent
   b. 46 percent
   c. 55 percent

Repeat the same procedure for Parts 2–5.

Part 2

3. How many young people were married in the 1960s?
   a. about 34 percent
   b. more than 50 percent
   c. over 80 percent

4. Why do some people wait to get married?
   a. They want to finish graduate school.
   b. They may have problems with the law.
   c. They can't get a college degree.

Part 3

5. Why are couples living outside of marriage "invisible in the statistics"?
   a. They count as single people.
   b. They do not have partners.
   c. They are not acceptable.

6. How many births were out of wedlock in the United States in 2008?
   a. 10 percent
   b. 20 percent
   c. 41 percent

7. Why are many young people choosing not to get married?
   a. They don't want to have children.
   b. They are too focused on the trends.
   c. The recession makes them insecure.

Part 4

8. Which of the following is true?
   a. Seventy percent of people have a college degree.
   b. Seventy-five percent of people with a college degree will never marry.
   c. Ninety percent of people with a college degree will marry.

9. According to Professor Andrew Cherlin, in the mid-20th century . . .
   a. not everybody got married.
   b. it was unusual for people to remain unmarried.
   c. less educated people did not marry.

Part 5

10. Americans who are having children out of wedlock . . .
    a. don't feel they need to be married.
    b. are trying to be like the Swedes or the French.
    c. are looking for stable relationships.

11. Cherlin says that in the United States, "living together relationships" . . .
    a. have the shortest duration of any country.
    b. tend to lead to marriage.
    c. will be like those in Sweden.

C. LISTENING AND MAKING INFERENCES

Listen to the excerpts and circle the best answers. Compare your answers with those of other students.

1. How does the interviewer, Melissa Block, respond to the data that show that most people will be married?
   a. She expected it.
   b. She is surprised by it.
   c. She cannot believe it.

2. How does Professor Andrew Cherlin feel about people cohabiting and not marrying in Europe?
   a. He is not affected by their decision.
   b. He is against their decision.
   c. He is supportive of their decision.

3. What does Cherlin think is the likelihood of the United States moving toward the Scandinavian patterns of long-term relationships outside of marriage?
   a. He is not sure whether it will happen.
   b. He thinks it will definitely happen.
   c. He thinks it won't happen.

IV. LOOKING AT LANGUAGE

A. USAGE: WORD FORMS

Notice Read the introduction to the interview. Notice the boldfaced words. Can these words be used as verbs? Think of examples.

Excerpt

And if you need any convincing that marriage is on the **decline** in the U.S., just take a **look** at new census numbers. They show a sharp **drop** in the married population, and an especially steep decline among young adults, ages 25 to 34. In that age **group**, the proportion of those never married climbed from 35 percent in 2000 to 46 percent now.

Explanation Many English words appear in the same form, whether they are nouns, verbs, or adjectives. In the four examples below, the noun form is the same as the base or infinitive form of the verb:

> *a decline / to decline*
>
> *a look / to look*
>
> *a drop / to drop*
>
> *a group / to group*

Other words may use the same form, but a change is made in pronunciation or syllable stress:

> *a REcord / to reCORD;*
>
> *an INcrease / to inCREASE*

Still other words have different noun and verb forms, such as:

> *an alternative / to alter*
>
> *a marriage / to marry*

Exercise 1

Work in pairs. Read the following excerpts from the interview. Identify the part of speech (noun, verb, etc.) of each boldfaced word, as it is used in the sentence. Write the part of speech above each word. The first one has been done for you.

1. We're going to **talk** *(verb)* about the **implications** of those numbers with Andrew

   Cherlin, sociology professor at Johns Hopkins and **author** of the book *The Marriage-Go-Round.*

2. For college-educated young adults, this is a story of postponing marriage.

   They want to finish **graduate** school, maybe have a couple of years as a law

   firm **associate** and then get married. So, they're waiting longer and longer until they have the rest of their lives in order before they get married.

3. And for everybody, we see an **increase** in couples living together outside of

   marriage.

4. And in recent years, how much to you think the **recession** is factoring into

   the **decision** or the **choice** not to get married?

5. So, even a **change** that says 20 to 25 percent of people might not get

   married in a certain **educational** group, even a change that modest is

   a huge change from the way marriage used to **dominate** adulthood in the U.S.

Exercise 2

Write the boldfaced words from Exercise 1 in the correct columns of the chart. If the word is a verb, write the base form. Then fill in the other forms of the word. Note the words that have the same form. The first one has been done for you.

NOUNS	VERBS	ADJECTIVES
talk	talk	talkative, talking

Exercise 3

Work in pairs. Use some of the words from the chart in Exercise 2 to talk about what you have learned about marriage in the United States. Use examples from your own culture to compare and contrast. An example has been provided for you.

Example:

A: Marriage is definitely on the decline in France. It seems no one gets married anymore.

B: In my country, people still marry, but they usually decide to marry after college.

B. PRONUNCIATION: SUFFIXES IN DIFFERENT WORD FORMS

Notice Listen to the following excerpt from the interview. Notice the pronunciation of the boldfaced words. What parts of speech are they? How is the pronunciation different in the verb form?

Excerpt

They want to finish **graduate** school, maybe have a couple of years as a law firm **associate** and then get married.

Explanation Many English words end with the suffix *-ate*. The pronunciation of the adjective form *graduate* is /ˈɡrædʒuɪt/, and of the noun form *associate* is /əˈsoʊʃiɪt/.

The pronunciation of the suffix changes, however, when the words are used as verbs. The verb form *graduate* is pronounced /ˈɡrædʒuˌeɪt/, and the verb *associate* is pronounced /əˈsoʊʃiˌeɪt/.

Exercise

Work in pairs. Identify the part of speech (noun, verb, etc.) of each boldfaced word as it is used in the sentence. Then take turns reading the sentences aloud. Use the correct suffix pronunciation based on the word's usage.

1. a. Business **associates** do not always share personal information about their family life with each other.

   b. Did you ever **associate** having a college degree with a having a higher chance of marrying?

2. a. Many couples put off marrying until they can **moderate** their expenses.

   b. Until couples can be sure of obtaining a **moderate** income, they may put off getting married.

3. a. The couple had to **deliberate** a long time before deciding to get married.

   b. The couple made a **deliberate** decision to have a baby before getting married.

4. a. Mid-20th century Americans were **advocates** for marriage.

   b. Today fewer Americans **advocate** for the necessity of marriage.

5. a. The cohabitation situation in Europe is **separate** from that in the United States.

   b. Americans living together as partners tend to **separate** after a few years.

6. a. A college **graduate** will have a greater chance of marrying than a non**graduate**.

   b. Many Americans wait until they **graduate** from college to marry.

7. a. It is difficult to **estimate** whether or not the United States will follow the trends of Sweden and France.

   b. The **estimate** of the number of less-educated people who will eventually marry is 75 to 80 percent.

8. a. Sweden is the **correlate** of France when it comes to the duration of long-term relationships.

   b. When we compare the U.S. marriage statistics from the 1960s to today, they do not **correlate**.

9. a. Professor Andrew Cherlin comments on the fact that Americans tend to break up or get married quickly, but he doesn't **elaborate** on that point.

   b. Some cultures are known for having grand weddings, with **elaborate** feasts and ceremonies.

10. a. Many young Americans **alternate** between partners before ever deciding to settle down and get married.

    b. In the mid-20th century, everybody got married. There was no **alternate** plan for couples in long-term relationships.

11. a. In the 1960s, Columbia University only admitted men. Barnard College was the **coordinate** college for women.

    b. In modern society, mothers and fathers have to carefully **coordinate** their work and home life in order to raise their children.

C. DISCOURSE ANALYSIS: SHOWING OBJECTIVITY

Notice **Listen to the following excerpts from the interview. How does the interviewee, Professor Andrew Cherlin, answer the interviewer's questions about marriage? What do you notice about the language he uses in these three examples? Does he give his opinion? Does he avoid giving his opinion? Comment on the differences between the three examples.**

Excerpt 1

Melissa Block: And let's put this in some context. If you look back at numbers from the 1960s, among this age group—young people, ages 25 to 34—more than 80 percent were married. Now we see that under 50 percent. What do you think is behind the slide?

Cherlin: For college-educated young adults, this is a story of postponing marriage. They want to finish graduate school, maybe have a couple of years as a law firm associate and then get married. So, they're waiting longer and longer until they have the rest of their lives in order before they get married.

Excerpt 2

Block: And in recent years, how much do you think the recession is factoring into the decision or the choice not to get married?

Cherlin: I think it's very important over the last year or two. These statistics have showed a very sharp drop in marriage, very recently in the last year or two, and that, I am sure, is because people are so insecure about their economic situation that they're not willing to tie the knot.

Excerpt 3

Block: Could you say, though, that if you look at the number of people who are living together and having children together outside of wedlock, that they may just be saying, we don't need to be married? We have the security we need. We have the family that we're starting in. We don't need the marriage certificate to get there.

Cherlin: And that's just the way many Europeans are. In countries like Sweden or France, there are lots of long-term cohabiting relationships lasting 10 or 20 or 30 years, and people say, why do we need to get married? Well, there is no reason, except so far, in this country, those living together relationships haven't lasted a long time.

Explanation In the interview, Cherlin only uses the first person "I" two times (Excerpt 2). Instead, he presents what he knows in the third person or occasionally uses the first person "we" to talk about the marriage situation. By doing this, Cherlin avoids giving his personal opinion, showing objectivity. His views are perhaps more convincing by presenting marriage statistics without focusing on what he believes.

Exercise

Work in pairs. Rewrite the excerpts in the Notice section on a separate piece of paper. Change Excerpts 1 and 3 to use the first person "*I*." Change Excerpt 2 to avoid the use of "*I*." Then read the excerpts aloud to the class. How do these changes affect the way the information is received?

V. FOLLOW-UP ACTIVITIES

A. DISCUSSION QUESTIONS

Work in groups. Discuss your answers to the questions.

In his book, *The Marriage-Go-Round*, Professor Andrew Cherlin writes the following about Americans' contradictory views about marriage and divorce:

> "When people think about the way marriage should be, they tend to say that it should be for life. But when people think about individual satisfaction, they tend to give others wide latitude to leave unhappy living arrangements."

1. In your own words, explain the meaning of the two opinions expressed in Cherlin's quote. Why do you think Americans have both of these opinions? What is your attitude about "the way marriage should be"?

2. What is your view of the growing numbers of unmarried, cohabiting couples? Do you think cohabiting couples can create successful families?

3. In some countries (Belgium, Canada, the Netherlands, Spain, some parts of the United States) same-sex marriages are allowed. Do you support same-sex marriages for your country?

B. DEBATE: IS MARRIAGE NECESSARY?

1. Take Notes to Prepare

Focusing on the facts about current marriage practices will prepare you to conduct a debate in the exercise that follows.

Listen to the interview again. Take notes on the issues concerning current marriage practices. Main topics and some examples have been provided for you.

Marriage is on the decline.

U.S. census - sharp drop in married population

_____

_____

_____

More and more unmarried couples are cohabiting.

Invisible – count as single people

_____

_____

_____

More children are born out of wedlock.

_____

_____

_____

_____

2. Consider the Issue

Divide into two teams to debate whether or not the institution of marriage should be preserved. Use your notes from Step 1 to help you prepare your argument.

Team A will argue in favor of the necessity of marriage.

You believe that marriage helps keep couples strong and families together. You think it is in the best interest of children to have married parents.

Team B will argue against the necessity of marriage.

You believe that marriage is no longer relevant. You think that couples can stay together and create strong families without being married.

3. Debate the Issue

Choose a moderator to lead the debate. The moderator will time the presentations and keep order during the debate. Follow the Debate Procedures below.

Debate Procedures

Preparation:

a. Each team meets separately to prepare a list of points to support its argument. (You may want to plan which team member will present which points during the debate.)

b. Each team tries to predict arguments that the other team will make; then it finds arguments against each of these.

Debate:

c. Team A and Team B sit facing each other. The moderator sits off to the side. (You may want to set a time frame for the whole debate.)

d. The moderator begins the debate by asking one of the teams to introduce the issue and to present the first argument in one minute or less.

e. A member of the opposing team responds in one minute or less. This back-and-forth format continues. After a member of one team has spoken, only a member of the opposing team may respond. Two members of the same team may not make arguments one after the other.

Wrap up:

f. The moderator announces when there are two minutes remaining, giving each team one final chance to make an argument.

g. At the end of the debate, the moderator evaluates the strength of each team's arguments.

"Tying the Knot" was first broadcast on All Things Considered, *September 29, 2010. The interviewer is Melissa Block.*

Answers to II. VOCABULARY, Exercise 1: 1. c   2. j   3. h   4. g   5. b   6. a   7. i   8. f   9. e   10. d

A Contribution to Make the World a Better Place

I. ANTICIPATING THE ISSUE

Discuss your answers to the questions.

1. From the picture and the title, discuss what you think the interview in this unit is about.

2. Many people dream of being wealthy. However, what disadvantages can you imagine there might be to having a lot of money?

3. If you had a lot of money, what would you want to do with it?

4. How would you like to be remembered by others?

Read the text. Use the context to help you understand the meaning of the boldfaced words and phrases. Write the number of each word or phrase next to its meaning at the end of the text.

A Brief Biography of George Soros

George Soros was born in Hungary in 1930. His father was a lawyer who liked living well, and Soros was raised in a comfortable, intellectual environment. But his life as a Hungarian Jew became difficult when the Nazis occupied Hungary in the 1940s. Assuming a false identity, Soros learned to survive on the streets by dealing with (1) **black marketers** who gave him his first lessons in learning the value of things. Amazingly, young George got through this difficult period (2) **unscathed**, and he looks back on his youth with fond memories. George Soros went to England in 1947 and attended the London School of Economics in 1952. It was there that he became aware of the sad condition of immigrants through his own life as an immigrant. While in England, Soros became familiar with the philosopher Karl Popper. Popper had a big influence on Soros's thinking and on his

decisions about donating money as a (3) **philanthropist**. Soros then moved to the United States to become one of the world's biggest (4) **financiers** of all time. In America, he began to build a large fortune as an institutional investor. By investing money in organizations or companies, such as banks and insurance companies, and by taking risks investing in (5) **hedge funds**, his own financial (6) **portfolio** grew larger and larger. Soon Soros became a multibillionaire and one of the most influential men in the world.

Soros recalls his earlier life saying, "I have prospered, but I know we all need a helping hand at some time in our lives." He established his first foundation, the Open Society Fund, in New York in 1979, his first European foundation in Hungary in 1984, and the Soros Foundation-Soviet Union in 1987. He now funds a network of foundations that operate in 31 countries. These foundations (7) **allocate** money toward the building and maintaining the basic systems and institutions of a free society. The responsibility he has assumed for others gives him a lot of influence, but it also gives him worries. He has even experienced (8) **psychosomatic illnesses** from managing other people's money.

Today, as a philosopher who has traded many (9) **commodities** in the world, Soros talks and writes about the (10) **perils** that could harm the world's economy.

He believes that the world is in the middle of a financial and political crisis. Soros points out that there are many (**11**) **dents** in today's global capitalist system. For example, international financial markets have been the main cause of failing economies. Clearly, capitalism has many (**12**) **drawbacks**. However, Soros's main (**13**) **pursuit** is to improve the operation of free markets to protect capitalistic societies.

_____ a. physical sicknesses caused by mental stress

_____ b. not hurt by a bad or dangerous situation

_____ c. small imperfections

_____ d. a collection of stocks owned by a particular person or company

_____ e. a rich person who gives money to help others

_____ f. products that are bought and sold

_____ g. decide to give a particular amount of money

_____ h. effort to attain a goal

_____ i. great dangers

_____ j. investment companies that take large risks in order to make a lot of money

_____ k. people who control or lend large sums of money

_____ l. significant negative effects

_____ m. people who buy and sell goods illegally

III. LISTENING

A. LISTENING FOR MAIN IDEAS

Listen to the interview. After each of the five parts, you will hear a beep. Write the main idea in a complete sentence, using the key word or phrase given. Then compare your sentences with those of another student. The first one has been done for you.

Part 1   multibillionaire

Multibillionaire and philanthropist George Soros became one of the world's

wealthiest men through his work as a financier.

Part 2   anxious

_____

_____

B. LISTENING FOR DETAILS

Read the questions for Part 1. Then listen to Part 1 again and circle the best answers. Compare your answers with those of another student. If your answers are different, listen again.

Part 1

1. What is special about Tuesdays in April on *Morning Edition*?
   a. The program will discuss taxes.
   b. The program will focus on money.
   c. The program will interview rich people.

2. How is George Soros described?
   a. a millionaire
   b. a financier
   c. a philosopher

3. Which of the following is NOT true about Soros?
   a. He is still working.
   b. He ran a hedge fund.
   c. He bought stocks and bonds.

Repeat the same procedure for Parts 2–5.

Part 2

4. What's the problem with managing people's money, according to Soros?
   a. You can't take risks with someone else's money.
   b. You can lose people's money.
   c. People want their money back.

5. What negative effect might Soros's currency trading[1] have caused, according to Stamberg?
    a. a stock market crash on Wall Street
    b. Asia's financial crisis
    c. more charges from financial companies

6. Which of the following is NOT true about Soros's background?
    a. He was born in Budapest.
    b. His father was a financier.
    c. He studied economics in school.

Part 3

7. Which of the following is true about the 14-year-old George Soros?
    a. He assumed a Jewish identity.
    b. He lived underground (in secret).
    c. He was suspected of carrying currency.

8. What lesson did George learn when he tried to trade?
    a. Sellers' estimates were usually reliable.
    b. His goods were not worth anything.
    c. The price of gold could go up and down.

9. How did young George feel about his experiences?
    a. They were frightening.
    b. They were a gift.
    c. Fighting evil made him suffer.

Part 4

10. Which of the following is true about Soros?
    a. He fought the communists.
    b. He left Hungary in 1946.
    c. He arrived in America with $5,000 in his pocket.

11. Which of the following describes Soros's "plan" after arriving in America?
    a. He would make a million dollars in one year.
    b. He would live on $15,000 a year.
    c. He would become a philosopher.

12. How would Soros have liked to be appreciated by others?
    a. as a person who could make a lot of money
    b. as someone with interesting ideas
    c. as someone who could talk about the stock market

---

[1]*currency trading:* the buying and selling of different moneys of the world

13. What does Soros think is fascinating?
    a. the pursuit of money
    b. the anticipation of the future
    c. what money can buy

14. What does having money allow Soros to do?
    a. focus on buying expensive things
    b. own a private plane and boat
    c. pursue his ideas

Part 5

15. How does Soros react to the idea that he is "saving the world"?
    a. He rejects it totally.
    b. He thinks it's very amusing.
    c. He agrees with it.

16. Which of the following is NOT correct in terms of the numbers?
    a. His foundations allocate half a billion dollars a year.
    b. His foundations allocate money to 31 countries.
    c. He has changed the lives of hundreds of people.

17. How does Soros feel about giving money?
    a. He gives money to people on the street.
    b. He looks for personal gratitude.
    c. He likes meeting people who have received his money.

18. How would Soros like to be remembered?
    a. as an author who has contributed to the world of finance
    b. as a financier who helped many people
    c. as a philosopher trying to understand life

C. LISTENING AND MAKING INFERENCES

Listen to the excerpts from the interview and answer the questions. Compare your answers with those of another student. If your answers are different, listen again.

1. Why does the interviewer, Susan Stamberg, say that Wall Street would have sent George Soros for "daily X-rays"?

   _____

2. What can you say about Soros's father's relationship with his son, George?

   _____

3. Why does Stamberg emphasize Soros's eye and hair color in her comment?

   _____

A. USAGE: PAST UNREAL CONDITIONAL

Notice   Listen to the following excerpt from the interview. Notice the boldfaced verb forms in the statement. Is the speaker talking about the present or the past?

Excerpt

Imagine if Wall Street **had known** that. They**'d have sent** him for daily X-rays.

Explanation   In the statement above, the interviewer imagines an unreal condition (Wall Street knowing about George Soros's backaches) and an unreal result of that condition in the past (giving him daily X-rays). The above statement can also be read as:

> Imagine if Wall Street **had known** that. They **would have sent** him for daily X-rays.

The past unreal conditional is generally formed as follows:

Condition Clause	Result Clause
If + subject + (*not*) **past perfect tense**	subject + **would/could/might** (**not**) **have** + past participle
If Wall Street **had known** about Soros's backaches,	they **would/could/might have sent** him for daily X-rays.
If Soros **had not had** backaches,	he **would/could/might not have known** that there was something wrong with his portfolio.

Exercise

Complete the sentences using information from the interview and your own ideas. Use the past unreal conditional in each sentence. The first one has been done for you.

1. If George Soros had not been responsible for other people's money,

   he would not have had anxiety and backaches.

2. If the Nazis had not invaded Hungary when George was a young boy,

   _____.

3. _____,

   it could have been more dangerous for young George to trade in currency.

4. If Soros had not accomplished his five-year plan, _____

   _____.

5. _____,
   Soros would not have been able to pursue his ideas.

6. _____,
   Soros would not have created foundations that allocate half a billion dollars a year.

B. PRONUNCIATION: CONTRACTED SPEECH

Notice   **Listen again to the excerpt from Part A. How is the underlined form pronounced in the result clause?**

Excerpt

Imagine if Wall Street had known that. They'<u>d</u> <u>have</u> sent <u>him</u> for daily X-rays.

Explanation   Contracted speech is a very natural form of speaking English. When students do not use the typical contractions that native speakers use, they often sound formal or unnatural.

In the example above, the auxiliary verb **would** is contracted to **'d**, and its pronunciation is reduced to a sound like /d/. The auxiliary verb **have** is also reduced. The /h/ sound is dropped, the vowel is reduced to /ə/, and the word **have** is pronounced like the word **of**. In spoken English, contractions are also commonly used after pronouns, as in the pronoun **him**, which is pronounced like /əm/.

The interviewer does not contract the use of **had** in the *if* clause of her first sentence. However, **had** is often contracted when used as an auxiliary in spoken English. Her sentence could have begun with: "Imagine if Wall Street**'d** known that." This form is normally not written.

Exercise 1

Go back to the sentences you wrote in Part A. Underline each of the auxiliary verbs that can be contracted. Write the contractions above the words. Then work with a partner. Take turns reading your sentences, focusing on the reduced forms.

Exercise 2

Work in pairs. Interview each other, asking the following questions. Answer using the unreal conditional. Pay attention to reducing the words *had*, *would*, and *have* in your questions and answers.

1. If you'd been born in your parents' generation, how would your life have been different?

2. If you could have added a sister or brother to your family, which would you have chosen?

3. If you'd listened more to your parents when you were young, what different decisions would you have made?

4. If your family had had more or less money, how would it have affected your life?

5. If you had been born George Soros, what would you have done differently from him?

C. DISCOURSE ANALYSIS: POWER AND ROLES IN DISCOURSE

Notice Listen to the following excerpt from the interview. What can you say about the way this part of the conversation develops?

Excerpt

Susan Stamberg: So when you went to sell it, they said, "Oh, but look at this thing. It's full of dents. It's awful. It's not worth anything."

George Soros: That's right. That's right.

Stamberg: You learned that.

Soros: That's right.

Stamberg: But you also learned about gold being a commodity.

Soros: Right. Right. That's right.

Stamberg: So they gave you that idea.

Soros: Well, of course.

Stamberg: And that the price of it could go up and down.

Soros: Right. Right.

Explanation Participants in interviews or conversations can affect discourse in different ways. This shaping can depend on power and roles. One's position in the world can determine whether or not he or she is empowered or has a voice. Power, competition, and gender roles can also affect discourse. The equality or inequality of speakers also influences the interchange of ideas.

In the excerpt above, the interviewer does not ask questions. Instead, she presents points about Soros's life in statement form, and he agrees with what she says. This type of exchange could be perceived as a power shift. One of the world's wealthiest men gives up his power, at least momentarily, as the interviewer directs the conversation.

Exercise 1

Work in pairs. Read the excerpt above. Then rewrite the dialogue on a separate piece of paper. Change the interviewer's statements to questions. Imagine how Soros would respond, and then write his answers. Discuss how the changes affect the discourse in the new conversation.

Exercise 2

At home, watch three minutes of an interview with a celebrity (on TV or online). Pay attention to power and roles of the interviewer and the interviewee. In the chart below, check (✓) each time you observe one of the interactions. (For example, for the excerpt in Exercise 1, Susan Stamberg would have five checkmarks under "Makes statement." George Soros would have five checkmarks under "Gives positive or negative response."

Bring your charts to class. In groups, discuss how different interview styles affect the conversation. What have you learned about power and roles?

INTERVIEWER (REPORTER)	INTERVIEWEE (CELEBRITY)
Asks question	Answers question with information
	Asks a question; redirects conversation
Makes statement	Gives positive or negative response
	Gives positive or negative response and adds information

V. FOLLOW-UP ACTIVITIES

A. DISCUSSION QUESTIONS

Work in groups. Discuss your answers to the questions.

1. Why does George Soros say he doesn't need a private plane or boat? What needs does he have? Why do you think he says this?

2. What kinds of life experiences help people toward success? Consider the life of George Soros and discuss any of his life experiences that seem to be common among successful people.

B. VALUES CLARIFICATION: THE VALUES OF A PHILANTHROPIST

1. Take Notes to Prepare

Focusing on George Soros's life experiences will prepare you react to the importance of his foundations' projects.

Listen to the interview again. Take notes on experiences from Soros's life that may have led to his role as a philanthropist. Main topics and an example have been provided for you. Use your notes to help you in the values clarification exercise that follows.

Soros's physical effects from managing other people's money:

made him anxious

_____

_____

_____

_____

His life as a 14-year-old boy:

_____

_____

_____

_____

Coming to America:

_____

_____

_____

_____

His personal values today:

What he wants:

_____

_____

_____

What he doesn't want:

_____

_____

_____

2. Consider the Issue

Work in groups. Read the following descriptions of projects of George Soros's Open Society Foundation. Consider the purpose and goal of each project. Based on the interview with Soros, which of these projects do you think best reflects Soros's values?

_____ **Justice Initiative**
This project promotes human rights for people around the world. The program offers legal and technical support to 1) help fight racial discrimination; 2) support criminal justice reform; 3) prevent abuse related to the fight against terrorism; 4) expand freedom of information and expression; and 5) fight dishonesty related to the use of natural resources.

_____ **Youth Initiative**
This project encourages young people to learn about and get involved in international policy issues that will affect their future. Global debates have been established in over 50 countries, with a particular focus on the Middle East and North Africa, China and Southeast Asia, Latin America, sub-Saharan Africa, and Central Asia. The project has also developed a media literacy curriculum to help young people analyze how they perceive and use the media.

_____ **Information Program**
The goal of this program is to increase access to knowledge and to protect the freedom to communicate in the digital environment, particularly in less developed parts of the world. Program activities include helping make legal information freely available online in 18 southern African countries, helping libraries provide electronic information worldwide, and increasing access to government information and decision making.

International Migration Initiative

_____ This program addresses the discrimination of migrants[2] during and after their journey to their country of destination. The program supports the quality of life for migrants around the world by addressing policy concerns and offering legal support. Its main goals are improving fairness in migration policy, and promoting equality and justice for migrants.

Global Drug Policy Program

_____ Fighting the drug problem with the criminal justice system is expensive and does not work. This program shifts the policy of fighting drugs from a crime-and-punishment issue to a health issue. Military strategies, such as spraying drug-producing plant crops, have hurt communities and damaged the environment. The program aims to reform international and national drug laws in an effort to respect human rights.

The Documentary Photography Project

_____ This project supports the use of photography as a tool for educating the public on human rights issues and social injustice around the world. Some themes of traveling photography exhibits have included: statelessness[3] of Nubians in Kenya, energy consumption in America, HIV-positive senior citizens, and socioeconomic challenges of young women in Troy, New York. Money from this fund supports photographers from regions that lack training or professional opportunities.

3. Group Discussion

With your group, consider the problems of your own communities. Decide which of the projects from Step 2 would benefit people in your city or town the most. Rank them from _1_ (most important) to _6_ (least important).

_____

[2]_migrants:_ people who move from one place to another
[3]_statelessness:_ not being considered as a national by any state through its nationality legislation or constitution

"_A Contribution to Make the World a Better Place_" was first broadcast on Morning Edition, _April 3, 2001._ _The interviewer is Susan Stamberg._

No Deal on Whales

I. ANTICIPATING THE ISSUE

Discuss your answers to the questions.

1. From the title and picture, what do you think the report in this unit is about?

2. What do you know about the history of whaling? What were whales hunted for in the past? What are they hunted for today?

3. What are the most pressing concerns involving international waters? What problems have developed in international waters as a result of globalization?

Use the context to help you understand the meaning of the boldfaced words and phrases. Write the number of each word or phrase next to its meaning at the end of the text.

1. There has been a **moratorium** on killing whales for more than two decades.

2. The halibut fishing industry suffered greatly in the late 20th century, but in recent years it has been **thriving**.

3. The sperm whale has become the **poster child** for protecting endangered wildlife in our oceans.

4. The national **sovereignty** of the United States was only achieved after many years of conflict and war with the British.

5. Many restaurants now serve food that is **sustainable**: Their chefs only use local produce that is grown in a safe, natural way.

6. Although some countries claim that they hunt whales only for scientific purposes, many people **allege** that they are hunting whales for food.

7. Under the **guise** of conducting market research, the telemarketer tried to get me to buy a new magazine subscription.

8. Before the famous Exxon Valdez oil spill, Alaska had been considered a **sanctuary** for sea life such as sea otters, seals, and seabirds.

9. Hunting whales for oil was a common practice of the past that became **obsolete** by the turn of the 20th century.

10. One of the biggest problems in the oceans is the unnecessary killing of fish and other sea life that get **entangled** in fishermen's nets.

11. The tourists on the cruise ship were **awed by** the display of whales breaching[1] in the ocean.

12. This year, the United Nations has a specific **reform agenda** focusing on economy, accountability, integrity, and excellence.

_____ a. having independent rule/authority over a territory

_____ b. capable of being continued without long-term negative effects on the environment

_____ c. twisted together in a confusing mass

_____ d. false appearance

_____ e. a list of changes or improvements which a group wants to make

_____ f. person or character used as a symbol to promote a cause

---

[1]*breaching:* leaping out of the water

_____ g. a waiting period set by an authority

_____ h. improving; growing; prospering

_____ i. inspired by a feeling of fear, wonder, or respect

_____ j. declare to be true before proof; affirm; assert

_____ k. no longer in general use

_____ l. a safe place where wildlife can be protected

III. LISTENING

A. LISTENING FOR MAIN IDEAS

Listen to the report. After each of the five parts, you will hear a beep. Write the main idea in a complete sentence, using the key word or phrase given. Then compare your sentences with those of another student.

Part 1 International Whaling Commission

_____

_____

Part 2 whale-watching trips

_____

_____

Part 3 whaling in Norway

_____

_____

Part 4 Australia alleges

_____

_____

Part 5 IWC Agreement

_____

_____

B. LISTENING FOR DETAILS

Read the statements for Part 1. Then listen to Part 1 again and write *T* (true) or *F* (false). Compare your answers with those of another student. If your answers are different, listen again.

Part 1

_____ 1. Madeira is in Portugal.

_____ 2. Whaling continues to be practiced in Madeira.

_____ 3. A moratorium on commercial whaling was established in 1986.

_____ 4. Whales are still hunted in Iceland.

_____ 5. Delegates from 18 countries are at this week's meeting.

Repeat the same procedure for Parts 2–5.

Part 2

_____ 6. The boat has two powerful motors.

_____ 7. There are 12 tourists on the trip.

_____ 8. The boat trip has to travel through rough waters.

_____ 9. These boat trips often disturb the sea mammals.

_____ 10. The boats keep a distance from the animals.

Part 3

_____ 11. Thousands of sperm whales have been harpooned[2] since the ban.

_____ 12. Today Madeira is the poster child for saving whales.

---

[2]*harpooned:* killed by spearfishing

_____ 13. Norway's commissioner says that whaling is important for Norway.

_____ 14. Norway is a big resource-utilization nation.

_____ 15. It is important to utilize whales in a sustainable way in Norway.

Part 4

_____ 16. Norway alone accounts for half of the 2,000 whales killed annually.

_____ 17. Japan kills the other 1,000 whales.

_____ 18. Donna Petrachenko believes that the International Whaling Commission needs to do more commercial whaling.

_____ 19. The IWC Organization has changed since it was started in 1946.

_____ 20. Climate change and collisions with ships are current concerns of the IWC.

_____ 21. About 30,000 dolphins and whales are killed each year by fishing nets.

Part 5

_____ 22. The sperm whales thrust their tails high above the water.

_____ 23. There has been a 23-year ban on whaling.

_____ 24. The organization may fall apart because its members cannot agree.

C. LISTENING AND MAKING INFERENCES

Listen to the excerpts from the report and circle the best answers. Compare your answers with those of other students.

1. What does Norway's commissioner say is the main purpose of whaling in Norway?
   a. to make money
   b. to compete with other whaling countries
   c. to do scientific research

2. What view does the reporter have toward Australia's position?
   a. He thinks it is silly.
   b. He agrees with it.
   c. He thinks it is too strong.

3. What is Donna Petrachenko's view of the organization?
   a. It will change.
   b. It needs to change.
   c. It will never change.

A. USAGE: NOUN CLAUSES IN SUBJECT POSITION

Notice   Listen to the excerpts from the report. Notice the boldfaced group of words that form the subject and complement in each sentence. How are they formed?

Excerpt 1

Why we are doing whaling is because we are a big resource-utilization nation, and for us to be able to utilize the natural resources in a sustainable, scientifically-based way is extremely important.

Excerpt 2

That's **why we come here with a reform agenda**: to change the focus of the IWC, to modernize it.

Explanation   In the example sentences above, noun clauses are used as a subject (Excerpt 1) and as a complement (Excerpt 2). A noun clause is a group of words consisting of a question word (*who, where, why,* etc.), a subject, and a verb. A noun clause acts as a *singular* subject.

In Excerpt 1 above, a noun clause is used as the subject of the sentence:

question word	subject	verb	
Why	*we*	*are*	*doing whaling*

In Excerpt 2, a noun clause forms the complement:

question word	subject	verb	
why	*we*	*come*	*here with a reform agenda*

In a noun clause, the subject precedes the verb. Question word order is NOT used in a noun clause. The question words *does, did,* and *do* are not used in noun clauses.

Correct: *Why we continue whaling . . .*

Incorrect: ~~*Why do we continue whaling*~~ *. . .*

If a statement answers a *yes/no* question, the word *whether* is used in the noun clause.

Do other countries kill whales?

Whether *other countries kill whales is not certain.*

Exercise

Read the excerpts from the interview. Then answer the questions using a noun clause in subject position. Use the information in the excerpt to answer the question. In sentences 5 and 10, you should answer with your own opinion. The first one has been done for you.

1. This week, the International Whaling Commission met on the Portuguese island of Madeira.

   Q: Where did they meet?

   A: Where *they met was on the Portuguese island of Madeira* _____.

2. But despite a 1986 moratorium on commercial whaling, Japan, Iceland, and Norway have all continued to hunt whales.

   Q: Where are whales still hunted?

   A: Where _____.

3. As Jerome Socolovsky reports, at this week's meeting, delegates from more than 80 countries have been unable to bridge their differences.

   Q: What have the delegates been unable to do?

   A: What _____.

4. Why we are doing whaling is because we are a big resource-utilization nation, and for us to be able to utilize the natural resources in a sustainable, scientifically-based way is extremely important.

   Q: Why is Norway whaling?

   A: Why _____.

5. Japan says that it kills the other 1,000 for what it calls scientific research.

   Q: Does Japan kill whales for only scientific research?

   A: Whether _____.

6. Donna Petrachenko represents Australia at the whaling commission.

   Q: Who does Petrachenko represent at the whaling commission?

   A: Who _____.

7. That's why we come here with a reform agenda: to change the focus of the IWC, to modernize it.

   Q: Why do they come with a reform agenda?

   A: Why _____.

8. Back on the inflatable boat, the passengers are awed by the sight of gigantic sperm whales.

   Q: What are the passengers awed by?

   A: What _____.

9. Frenchman Emil Sassa says he thinks it's a crime that whaling continues despite the 23-year-old ban.

Q: Who does the reporter speak to?

A: Who _____.

10. The IWC members have given themselves another year to reach some kind of agreement. If they fail, observers say the organization will likely fall apart.

Q: Will the organization reach an agreement?

A: Whether _____.

B. PRONUNCIATION: THOUGHT GROUPS

Notice Listen to the excerpt. Why do you think the groups of words below have been separated? How does the speaker say these words?

Excerpt

Why we are doing whaling / is / because we are a big resource-utilization nation, / and for us to be able to utilize the natural resources / in a sustainable, / scientifically-based way / is extremely important.

Explanation When we speak, we group words together and join the groups into sentences. These groups are called "thought groups." They help the listener organize the meaning of the sentence. For example, the noun clause in the subject position of the sentence above is spoken as one thought group. Short noun clauses are usually said as one thought group.

Notice that short noun clauses in subject position, as the one above, normally form one thought group while longer noun clauses in subject position normally form more than one thought group.

When reading text, it is often easy to see a thought group. Punctuation, such as commas and periods, shows us where thought groups begin and end.

As Jerome Socolovsky reports, / at this week's meeting, / delegates from more than 80 countries / have been unable to bridge their differences.

When speaking, we naturally pause when whole ideas are expressed, usually after prepositional phrases, noun phrases, verb phrases, and short clauses:

Correct: *Karsten Klepsvik / will be interviewed / on tomorrow's program.*

Incorrect: ~~Karsten / Klepsvik / will be interviewed on / tomorrow's program.~~

Pausing between different groups of words can change the meaning of a sentence. Notice the different meaning for the following sentences. In the first example, Jerome Socolovsky is a popular person; his job is radio station reporter.

In the second sentence, Jerome Socolovsky is a reporter on a radio station that is popular.

> *Jerome Socolovsky is a / popular / radio station reporter.*
>
> *Jerome Socolovsky is a / popular radio station / reporter.*

Exercise 1

Go back to the sentences you wrote in Part A on page 123. Draw slashes (/) in between each thought group in your sentences. Read your sentences aloud to a partner.

Exercise 2

Listen to the excerpts from the report. Some punctuation has been removed. Draw slashes (/) between the thought groups that you hear in each statement.

1. But despite a 1986 moratorium on commercial whaling Japan Iceland and Norway have all continued to hunt whales.

2. An inflatable boat with two powerful motors glides slowly out of Madeira's Funchal Harbor carrying a dozen tourists on a whale-watching trip.

3. Australia believes you don't need to kill a whale to do proper science.

4. We've looked at the organization which you know has its origins in 1946 and the world was very, very different in 1946 than in 2009.

Exercise 3

Work in pairs. Student A, choose one of the sentences in the left column and read it aloud. Use the commas in the sentences to pause between thought groups. Student B, listen and say the correct response from the right column. Change roles after item 4.

Student A	Student B
1. a. The tourists went whale watching on a pretty clear day. b. The tourists went whale watching on a pretty, clear day.	a. It was a beautiful day. b. There were a few clouds.
2. a. The deep blue waters of the Atlantic were like a mirror. b. The deep, blue waters of the Atlantic were like a mirror.	a. The waters are deep. b. The color blue is dark.
3. a. Tourists can enjoy viewing the huge ocean animals and clear sky. b. Tourists can enjoy viewing the huge ocean, animals, and clear sky.	a. They enjoy two things. b. They enjoy three things.
4. a. Jerome said Alicia is interested in whales. b. "Jerome," said Alicia, "is interested in whales."	a. Jerome is interested in whales. b. Alicia is interested in whales.

Change roles.

	Student A	**Student B**
5.	a. Norway has a big, fish industry. b. Norway has a big fish industry.	a. Norway sells a lot of fish. b. Norway sells large fish.
6.	a. I know where two countries are doing commercial whaling in Norway and Japan. b. I know where two countries are doing commercial whaling: in Norway and Japan.	a. Norway and Japan are doing commercial whaling. b. Two other countries are doing commercial whaling in Norway and Japan.
7.	a. Out toward the sunset, there's a great whale watch. b. Out toward the sunset, there's a great whale. . . . Watch!	a. There is a very big whale to observe. b. There is a boat with people watching whales.
8.	a. Look at the whale that is fast. b. Look at the whale. That is fast.	a. There are several whales. One is fast. b. There is one whale to look at. He is fast.

C. DISCOURSE ANALYSIS: SPEAKER'S STANCE

Notice   **Listen to the excerpt from the report. Which words in the statement give a hint about the reporter's opinion? How might these words influence the listener's attitude toward what he is reporting?**

Excerpt

Japan says it kills the other 1,000 for what it calls scientific research.

Explanation   The reporter uses reported speech, "Japan says . . . ," to explain Japan's claims about killing whales. By including the phrase "what it calls" in the statement, the reporter is also expressing his own (and/or the radio station's) stance, or opinion. By choosing this phrase, he seems to be questioning the truthfulness about Japan's killing whales for scientific research. He is saying, "Japan *calls* it scientific research, but it's really something else."

Exercise

At home, listen to a radio report. Find examples of reported speech in which the reporter qualifies what is reported. How does his or her choice of language reflect his or her personal opinion?

A. DISCUSSION QUESTIONS

Work in groups. Discuss your answers to the questions.

1. Do you agree with Commissioner Karsten Klepsvik from Norway, that whaling is about national sovereignty? Or, do you agree with the tourist from France, that it is a crime that whaling continues?

2. Norway is historically more dependent on whaling than other nations, which may explain Klepsvik's argument for national sovereignty. What other issues of national sovereignty exist in today's world? Give examples and express your opinions about the arguments made for national sovereignty.

B. VALUES CLARIFICATION: INTERNATIONAL WATERS

1. Take Notes to Prepare

Focusing on issues expressed in the report about whaling will prepare you to judge the importance of other issues that involve international waters.

Listen to the interview again. Take notes on whaling issues expressed in the report. Main topics and some examples have been provided for you. Listen again if necessary. Use your notes to help you in the exercise that follows.

Whale-watching industry:

- *sperm whales in north Atlantic* _____
- _____
- *keep a distance from the animals* _____
- _____

Pro-whaling:

- _____
- _____
- *sustainable, scientifically-based way* _____
- _____
- *Japan kills other half for research* _____

Anti-whaling:

- *anti-whaling bloc, lead by Australia*

- _____

- *need to focus on conservation, not commercial whaling*

- *need to focus on other threats*

- *climate change*

- _____

- _____

- *300,000 per year*

- *Frenchman: it's a crime*

Future of the IWC:

- _____

- *if not, organization may fall apart*

2. Consider the Issue

Work in groups. Each student is a representative of a different country concerned about the earth's international waters. Choose a country to represent. (This can be your home country, a country in which you have lived or spent time, or a country that you know well.) Consider your country's position on the following issues involving international waters.

_____ **Whaling industry**

Traditionally, whales were hunted for meat and oil. Since 1986, however, there has been a moratorium on commercial whaling as whales are now considered to be an endangered species. Some countries, such as Iceland, Japan, and Norway, insist that whaling must continue for scientific reasons. They also focus on the sovereignty of traditional whaling countries. But countries such as Australia insist that the only way whales should be commercialized today is for ecotourism. Pro-whaling countries believe that the ban on whaling has already restored the whale population in our oceans. Antiwhaling countries and environmental groups continue to claim that whales are an endangered species and that whaling should be banned.

Crime on the seas

Pirates are not a thing of the past. Modern pirates, such as those on the coast of Somalia, have posed a huge threat to our international waters. They have interrupted international commerce, held merchant sailors hostage, and killed many innocent people. They prevent food aid from reaching its destinations. There have been many incidents over the past decade in which pirates, using small, fast boats, have attacked bigger cargo ships. They do not steal the cargo, but they rob the crew and take anything of value off the ship. In international waters, crew members are not legally able to protect themselves with guns or other weapons. They are very easy targets.

Ocean traffic

Historically, sailors have had the freedom to navigate the open seas. But in recent decades there has been an increase in the number of large merchant ships traveling over the oceans. Collisions have become more frequent because of heavy boat traffic. Not only do ship passengers get killed, but there are more and more collisions between whales and merchant ships with such high traffic in the oceans.

Environmental issues/Climate change

It is now clear that most of the global warming over the last 50 years is likely to have been related to human activity. As the earth warms, sea levels rise. This affects coastal areas. Human activity also pollutes the earth's oceans. Dumping waste into the oceans causes the death of sea life. Oil spills lead to disappearing coral reefs and endangered species. The oceans are also used for shipping dangerous substances and weapons overseas. For example, many worry about the consequences of an accident possibly involving a shipment of plutonium overseas.

Overfishing

Eighty percent of life on earth is in our oceans, but overfishing poses one of the most significant threats to the world. The oceans contained six times more fish in 1900 than they do today. Over 70 percent of the world's fisheries have been over-exploited, completely used up, or put out of business. Ninety percent of the large, predatory fish stocks, including tuna and cod, are now gone. The oceans provide an essential food source for many people. Over two hundred million people, primarily in the developing world, depend on our oceans for their livelihood, but the fish are disappearing.

Rights to ocean development

A coastal nation has sovereign rights for exploring, exploiting, or conserving the ocean as far as 200 miles from shore. Beyond that point, international law considers the ocean to be "high seas," where all nations have certain freedoms to navigate, travel, harvest fish, lay cables and pipelines, and conduct scientific research. Sixty percent of the world's oceans fall into this category.

As the world competes for more resources such as oil, disputes have grown over whether particular waters are international waters. For example, Russia, Norway, Canada, and Denmark view the Arctic Ocean as national waters while the United States and most European countries regard the Arctic as international waters. As the world becomes more globalized, so will the disputes over who has rights to these international waters.

3. Group Discussion

With your group, decide which of the threats from Step 2 need the most attention right now. Rank them from most important (1) to least important (6) in solving the current problems of international waters. Discuss your opinions and try to agree with the representatives in your group.

"No Deal on Whales" was first broadcast on All Things Considered, *June 26, 2009. The reporter is Jerome Socolovsky.*

Is It a Sculpture, or Is It Food?

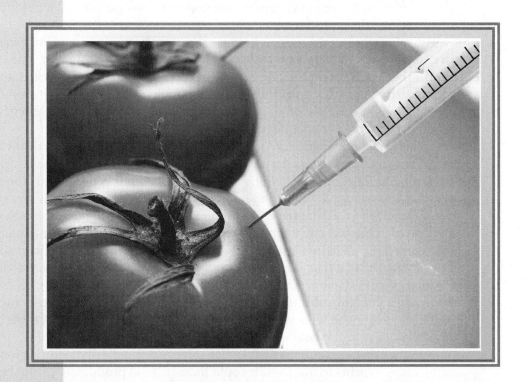

Discuss your answers to the questions.

1. From the title and the picture, discuss what you think the interview in this unit is about.

2. When you buy fruits and vegetables, what is important to you: taste, texture, color, nutrition, price, or how long something stays fresh? Why?

3. Genetically engineered foods (also known as genetically modified or GMOs) are foods that are scientifically altered to produce more, grow faster, or last longer. Have you ever eaten food that was genetically engineered? What was it? How did you know it was genetically engineered? What did it look like? How did it taste?

Read the text. Use the context to help you understand the meaning of the boldfaced words and phrases. Write the number of each word or phrase next to its meaning at the end of the text.

Experiments in genetic engineering have created important (1) **breakthroughs** in many areas; they have led to cures for many diseases, the control of insect populations, and the improvement of food production. However, most of these experiments are not (2) **foolproof**; no one knows for sure what negative consequences they could have.

Imagine what might happen to genes that have been genetically engineered in scientists' laboratories once they are released into the environment. The (3) **ramifications** of introducing these genes could be terrifying. People sometimes (4) **poke fun at** progress, possibly because technology often creates new problems as it attempts to solve old ones. In fact, some people have a name for genetically manipulated food: "Frankenfood."

Whether or not the fear of "science-fiction food" is realistic, genetically engineered food has received a great deal of attention recently because many of these food products are now on the market. For example, gene-spliced fruits and vegetables have been developed to improve their color, taste, and shelf life. Some people are concerned that these foods don't taste the same as natural foods, or that the process used to create them may cause people to become sick. For instance, in order to create a longer lasting tomato, scientists have mixed genetic material from tomatoes with that of the common freshwater fish, trout. People who have (5) **allergies** to fish may become ill eating these tomatoes if the trout gene has not been sufficiently (6) **sublimated** in the gene-splicing process. Restaurant owners, as well as others who work with food, have organized a (7) **boycott** of these foods to show their disagreement with this type of food production.

On the other hand, many people recognize that genetically modified food can bring many benefits to our lives. It could increase food production throughout the world and begin to solve the hunger problem. It could improve the taste and shelf life of many foods. Genetically engineered food could also (8) **alleviate** our dependence on pesticides to protect crops; if fewer pesticides were used, the problem of pesticide (9) **residue** in food could be reduced. Finally, these foods could provide a (10) **boon** to the food industry, which could help the (11) **fragile** world economy.

Most people will agree that more information is needed before we can be sure whether genetically engineered food will improve our lives. We need to weigh the advantages with the disadvantages, as well as consider the dangers, before we make further commitments to experimenting in this area.

_____ a. rapid increase or expansion

_____ b. certain to be successful; always effective

_____ c. abnormal sensitivities to certain foods or other substances

_____ d. new discoveries

_____ e. blended; weakened

_____ f. something remaining; part of something that is left behind

_____ g. easily damaged or ruined

_____ h. make better or less severe

_____ i. refusal to buy or use a product as a way of protesting

_____ j. results that affect other things

_____ k. joke about; make fun of

III. LISTENING

A. LISTENING FOR MAIN IDEAS

Listen to the interview. After each of the four parts, you will hear a beep. Write the main idea in a complete sentence, using the word or phrase given. Then compare your answers with those of another student.

Part 1 ➤ boycott

Chefs from around the country have organized a boycott of genetically

engineered food.

Part 2 ➤ the tomato

_____

_____

Part 3 ➤ public safety

_____

_____

Part 4 ➤ right to know

_____

_____

B. LISTENING FOR DETAILS

Read the statements for Part 1. Then listen to Part 1 again and write *T* (true) or *F* (false). Compare your answers with those of another student. If your answers are different, listen again

Part 1

At the time of the interview, . . .

_____ 1. genetically designed tomatoes are already available in the supermarket.

_____ 2. genetically engineered cheese can now be purchased.

_____ 3. genetic engineering can be used to create foods that are lower in fat.

_____ 4. over 1,000 chefs decided not to serve genetically engineered food.

_____ 5. special labeling is required for genetically engineered food.

Repeat the same procedure for Parts 2–4.

Part 2

Joyce Goldstein believes that . . .

_____ 6. genetic engineering is being used to improve the flavor of tomatoes.

_____ 7. the use of fish genes in tomatoes is a good idea.

_____ 8. genetically-engineered foods should be thoroughly tested and labeled before they are sold.

Part 3

According to Goldstein, . . .

_____ 9. the methods of the old days were better than those today.

_____ 10. genetically bred roses are very beautiful and smell good.

_____ 11. restaurants shouldn't serve genetically engineered food until it is tested.

_____ 12. we should worry more about corporate profit.

_____ 13. the Food and Drug Administration[1] does a good job of regulating these foods.

Part 4

According to Goldstein, . . .

_____ 14. pesticide residue in foods is a problem.

_____ 15. genetic manipulation of foods to reduce their dependence on pesticides is a good thing.

---

[1]*Food and Drug Administration:* government organization that regulates the sale and use of food and pharmaceutical drugs

_____ 16. the crossing of trout with tomatoes is a good thing.

_____ 17. genetic experimentation should help improve the taste of food.

_____ 18. what is good for agribusiness is generally good for the consumer.

_____ 19. consumers are given the information they need in purchasing food.

C. LISTENING AND MAKING INFERENCES

Listen to the excerpts and write answers to the questions. Compare your answers with those of other students.

1. How does Joyce Goldstein feel about "progress"? Why does she put it in quotes?

   _____

2. What is Goldstein's view of the Food and Drug Administration?

   _____

3. How sure is Goldstein that agribusiness will work toward making foods that are good for the consumer?

   _____

IV. LOOKING AT LANGUAGE

A. USAGE: PARALLEL STRUCTURE

Notice Listen to the following excerpt. Pay attention to the underlined phrases. How are they similar? What grammatical form do they all share?

Excerpt

In the near future, you might be able to buy <u>a tomato in the supermarket that has been genetically designed and engineered</u>, <u>a tomato that would stay ripe much longer</u>, <u>strawberries that are not so fragile in freezing temperatures</u>, <u>vegetable oil that's lower in fat.</u>

Explanation The sentence above is a good example of the use of parallel structure. The reporter lists four examples of what genetic engineering will be able to do. In each case, he uses noun phrase + restrictive adjective clause. For example:

Noun Phrase	**Restrictive Adjective Clause**
a tomato in the supermarket	*that has been genetically designed and engineered*

Parallel structure is very useful in both speaking and writing. When we use the same grammatical form in lists or groups of ideas, listeners can follow and remember what we say more easily. Parallel structure also gives text a more sophisticated style. For example:

In the future, it's likely that there will be <u>more research</u>, <u>more data</u>, and <u>more restrictions</u> on genetically modified foods.

Exercise

Listen to the excerpts. Underline the examples of parallel structure in each statement. Each group of words you underline should have the same grammatical structure.

1. Is it a sculpture, or is it food?

2. I guess the thing is, when a new product comes on the market like this, number one, you'd like to be aware that it's being sold to you, and number two, you'd like to know that they have checked out all of these ramifications before they put it on the shelf.

3. All I'm saying is, right now we have a lot of nonknowledge about this stuff, and until things are tested and until we know what they taste like and how they are, we don't want to put them on the menu.

4. I think we just need to see a little bit more data on this, and I think it's too soon to tell.

5. When you read that these things are happening, and you know that the first person that it's good for is agribusiness, and then you wonder . . .

B. PRONUNCIATION: LISTING INTONATION

Notice   **Listen to the same sample excerpt from Part A on page 135. Pay attention to the list of foods that the reporter says may be sold in the future. Notice the intonation patterns of the underlined words and phrases. When is there a falling intonation? When is there a rising intonation? Why?**

Excerpt

In the near future, you might be able to buy <u>a tomato in the supermarket that has been genetically designed and engineered</u>, <u>a tomato that would stay ripe much longer</u>, <u>strawberries that are not so fragile in freezing temperatures</u>, <u>vegetable oil that's lower in fat</u>.

Explanation   When speakers list items, they tend to use a rising intonation for each item until they finish. In the example above, this rising intonation indicates to the listener that the speaker could go on, or that there may be more examples that the speaker cannot think of. The list is unfinished.

The items on the list can be phrases, like those in the example on page 136, or they can be single words. Each item is pronounced together as a thought group.

If the list is finished, however, the last item has a rise-fall pattern. Generally, the conjunctions *and* or *or* introduce the final item of the list. Listen to the example sentence below. Listen for the rising intonation of each item before the last item. The last item has a rise-fall pattern to indicate that the speaker has finished.

The genetically-engineered foods that are mentioned in this interview are tomatoes, strawberries, oil, and cheese.

Exercise 1

Read the mini-dialogues. Is the speaker's list finished? Draw an intonation arrow (⌣↗ ⌢↘) for each underlined word and phrase. The first one has been done for you.

1. A: Which foods are being genetically designed these days?

   B: Primarily fruits and vegetables such as <u>tomatoes</u>, <u>strawberries</u>, <u>melons</u> . . .

2. A: Why are foods being genetically engineered?

   B: <u>To resist freezing temperatures</u>, <u>stay ripe longer</u>, and <u>maintain a longer shelf life</u>.

3. A: Why is Joyce Goldstein concerned about genetically-modified food?

   B: She is worried about <u>allergies</u>, <u>pesticides</u>, and <u>corporate profit</u>.

4. A: What are the effects of genetically engineering food?

   B: The food is changed in terms of its <u>look</u>, <u>taste</u>, <u>smell</u> . . .

5. A: Which groups are expressing their views about genetically engineered food?

   B: Lots of people are voicing their opinions: <u>restaurant chefs</u>, <u>agribusiness</u>, <u>the Food and Drug Administration</u> . . .

6. A: What good points does Goldstein mention about genetically-altered roses?

   B: She says that <u>they're beautiful</u>, <u>they smell good</u>, and <u>they're safe</u>.

Exercise 2

Work in pairs. Practice reading the mini-dialogues in Exercise 1 with the correct intonation patterns. Change roles after item 3.

C. DISCOURSE ANALYSIS: THE PRONOUN *THEY*

Notice Listen to the excerpt from the interview. Notice the use of the pronoun *they*. Who is Joyce Goldstein referring to? Why doesn't she mention the subjects that these pronouns refer to?

Excerpt

When I first heard about it, I thought, well, **they**'re not even talking about flavor. The only thing **they**'re talking about is how long **they** can keep the damn thing on the shelf.

Explanation In the above example, Goldstein chooses not to specifically mention the subject of the sentence. Instead, she uses the pronoun *they* to keep the subject general and open. We can imagine that she is talking about those involved in agribusiness (those who make a profit from selling food) but she does not mention anyone directly. By using the pronoun *they*, she also distinguishes herself from another group of people. She contrasts her own interests from the interests of others.

Sometimes there is a clear reference for the use of the pronoun *they*. Sometimes there is not, as in the example above.

Exercise

Listen to more excerpts from the interview. As you listen, underline all the examples of the pronoun *they*. Then answer these questions with a partner:

- Is there a clear reference for *they* in the statement? If not, who do you think *they* refers to?

- Discuss the advantages and disadvantages of using *they* without a clear reference.

- Rephrase the statements by replacing *they* with specific subjects. How does it change the conversation?

1. **Joyce Goldstein:** You know, I mean, you worry how long they want to keep it. Is it a sculpture, or is it food? And I just kept thinking, I hope that we will get to find out more about this, and that they'll do some testing. For example, if they're using these trout genes in other products, and we have customers with fish allergies, are they going to get sick?

2. **Noah Adams:** There's the idea that they would use a fish gene to make tomatoes more frost resistant.

   Joyce Goldstein: Right.

3. **Goldstein:** Well, I mean, will people with fish allergies have responses to this, or will that be so sublimated that they won't have any effect? I guess the thing is, when a new product comes on the market like this, number one, you'd like to be aware that it's being sold to you, and number two, you'd like to know that they have checked out all of these ramifications before they put it on the shelf.

4. **Goldstein:** If they could come up with a wonderful product through genetic—I mean they have done, you know, wonderful roses with genetic breeding that are perfectly beautiful and still have some scent—if they could do this and prove it was safe to the public, I'm not going to say that it's a bad thing.

5. **Goldstein:** All I'm saying is, right now we have a lot of nonknowledge about this stuff, and until things are tested and until we know what they taste like and how they are, we don't want to put them on the menu.

6. **Adams:** There's an argument that's being made that this could be, I've seen one quotation, "the biggest boon to corporate profits since frozen food," that this could be that big a breakthrough in the food area.

   Goldstein: Well, I mean, they're always worrying about corporate profit. What if the stuff turns out not to be good?

7. **Goldstein:** I think that's a good thing. I'm just concerned when they start crossing trout with tomatoes as to what happens. I'm concerned. I will be delighted if they can make something taste wonderful and not have chemicals and pesticides. When you read that these things are happening, and you know that the first person that it's good for is agribusiness, and then you wonder, well, how good is it for the consumer, and that they will put these things at the market or try to sell it to us without letting us know, I think we have the right to know.

V. FOLLOW-UP ACTIVITIES

A. DISCUSSION QUESTIONS

Work in groups. Discuss your answers to the questions.

1. Should genetically engineered food be boycotted by restaurant owners, supermarket owners, consumers in general?

2. Should the government require special labeling for genetically engineered foods? If so, what information should be on the label?

3. Some people have called genetically engineered food "science-fiction food" or even "Frankenfood." Do you think human beings' manipulation of nature benefits or harms society? Can you think of other examples of human beings' manipulating nature? How do you feel about it?

B. ORAL PRESENTATION: BIOFOODS

1. Take Notes to Prepare

Focusing on Joyce Goldstein's concerns about genetically-engineered food will help you prepare questions for your research for the oral presentation that follows.

Listen to the interview again. Take notes on the benefits and disadvantages of genetic engineering. Main topics and some examples have been provided for you.

Benefits of genetic engineering:

- *tomato that stays ripe longer* _____
- *strawberries that are not so fragile* _____
- _____
- _____
- _____
- _____

Disadvantages of genetic engineering:

- *not about flavor* _____
- *no special labeling* _____
- _____
- _____
- _____
- _____

2. Oral Presentation

Prepare a five-minute oral presentation. Choose a country with which you are familiar. Research the current attitudes and practices regarding genetically-engineered food in that country. You may want to research the following issues raised about this food in the interview:

- longer shelf-life
- taste, appearance
- serving it in restaurants
- required labeling
- frost-resistance
- reduced dependence on pesticides
- relieving hunger
- government controls
- corporate profits
- public reactions

Follow the Oral Presentation Procedures below.

Oral Presentation Procedures

1. Choose a country that you know well or that you are interested in.

2. Use the Internet to look for current data on genetically-engineered food. Look for new discoveries, benefits and dangers, and regulations. Take notes.

3. Summarize your findings on an index card. You will refer to these notes when you give your presentation.

4. Create three to five PowerPoint™ slides to enhance your talk. Keep the text very brief. Use more images to support your presentation.

5. Practice your presentation at home. Give your presentation in front of friends or family members, or in front of the mirror. Time yourself for no more than five minutes.

6. Give your five-minute presentation in class. Be sure to include an introduction to the country you have chosen and its current position on genetically-engineered food. Present the data you have collected. Then, draw a conclusion to the use of genetically-engineered food in that country.

7. Follow the points in the box on the next page. Your teacher or classmates may want to rate your presentation according to content interest, organization, use of PowerPoint, pronunciation, fluency, grammar, and vocabulary.

"Is It a Sculpture, or Is It Food?" was first broadcast on All Things Considered, *August 3, 1992. The interviewer is Noah Adams.*

Preparing for Climate Change

I. ANTICIPATING THE ISSUE

Discuss your answers to the questions.

1. From the title and picture, what do you think the report in this unit is about?

2. What effects of climate change have you witnessed in your lifetime? Give examples.

3. Who do you think should be responsible for dealing with the problem of climate change?

Read the sentences in the box. Then read the numbered sentences below. After each numbered sentence, write the sentence from the box to create a mini-dialogue. Use a dictionary if necessary.

I agree. There are serious **repercussions** to continuing to burn fossil fuels.

He needs to **confront** her and explain why he thinks he is doing a good job.

You're right. And much of the world **famine** could be solved if there were better international relations.

It's possible. The Pentagon[1] has many **contingencies** in case of war.

It's clear that the media's **priorities** are selling news and making money.

Well, imagine the following **scenarios** from global warming: more hurricanes, floods, fires, and earthquakes.

Well, even though he's a **veteran**, he still has a strong connection to the military.

For one thing, like many other countries, it has put much more attention towards **national security**.

Yes, only **intelligence** officials in the C.I.A. would know about them.

If that happens, people will need to change their **mindset** about regional climates.

That is because they are afraid of **mass migrations** from neighboring countries that suffer from political instability.

And though that may be a good thing, those countries are now **destabilized,** with no leadership.

---

1. A: The government's involvement in those activities is top secret.

   B: _____

2. A: Those countries have such strict border patrols!

   B: _____

---

[1]*The Pentagon:* head office of the U.S. Department of Defense

3. A: It is predicted that because of global warming, North America's climate may get hotter while Europe's climate may get colder.

   B: _____

4. A: John never knows how to deal with his boss's complaints about his work.

   B: _____

5. A: Will the U.S. enlist more soldiers if the country is attacked?

   B: _____

6. A: Why does the TV news keep showing the picture of the politician with that woman?

   B: _____

7. A: I think the biggest problem in the world today is hunger.

   B: _____

8. A: Recently, people in many countries have forced bad leaders to leave office.

   B: _____

9. A: Even though he's been out of the army for many years, John continues to attend military functions.

   B: _____

10. A: I think we should work harder to find alternative energy sources.

   B: _____

11. A: I don't really see how a warmer climate will be so bad.

   B: _____

12. A: How has the United States changed since 9/11?

   B: _____

A. LISTENING FOR MAIN IDEAS

Listen to the report. After each of the five parts, you will hear a beep. Answer the question in a complete sentence. Then compare your answers with those of another student.

Part 1 How is climate change now being viewed by the U.S. government?

_____

_____

Part 2 Who plays an important role in confronting climate change?

_____

_____

Part 3 What kind of scenarios make climate change a security concern?

_____

_____

Part 4 What information will the Quadrennial Defense Review address?

_____

_____

Part 5 What concern does Professor James Carafano have about the military's preparations for climate change?

_____

_____

B. LISTENING FOR DETAILS

Read the sentences for Part 1. Listen to Part 1 again and fill in the blanks with the missing words or phrases. Compare your answers with those of another student. If your answers are different, listen again.

1. Within the U.S. government, climate change is the concern of the White

    House, _____, and the Pentagon.

2. The _____ agenda is pretty full these days.

3. Climate change has to _____ for attention.

Repeat the same procedure for Parts 2–5.

Part 2

4. Security experts don't bother evaluating the _____ about global warming.

5. A senior intelligence official says he assumes that the most likely outcome

    is the _____ . That's the intelligence view.

6. Military leaders prepare for _____.

7. The vast majority of _____ are convinced that climate

    change is a(n) _____.

8. The military plays an important role in _____ climate change.

Part 3

9. The reporter says that if the Himalayan glaciers melted, rivers fed by the

    glaciers would _____ at first, then _____ once the
    glaciers retreat.

10. That would _____ tens of millions of people around Bangladesh.

11. Retired Air Marshal A.K. Singh foresees _____ of people, with
    militaries becoming involved.

12. According to Singh, people would start fighting for _____

    and _____.

13. With migrations, the military would have to resolve _____.

14. Climate change is a security concern because of migrations, humanitarian

    _____, food and water shortages, and _____ over
    resources.

Part 4

15. The next Quadrennial Defense Review will address climate changes for the

    _____ ever.

16. Severe _____ events may increase in intensity in the future,

    and perhaps in _____ as well.

17. Retired Vice Admiral Lee Gunn makes the point that _____

    and _____ designers need to consider the climate in the future.

18. The Quadrennial Defense Review will say what _____ would

    mean for the _____ roles, missions, and installations.

19. Climate change may be a more important subject for intelligence analysts than

    for _____.

20. The C.I.A.'s Center for the Study of Climate Change is trying to predict where

    the next _____ might arise, or which countries are in most danger

    of being _____.

21. Professor James Carafano doesn't think we're very good at predicting

    _____ or _____.

22. Carafano agrees that climate change could have major security

    _____, but jumping to the wrong conclusions could be as

    dangerous as _____ climate change.

23. The bottom line is that national security officials should

    _____ future climate and security _____, whether
    they can do something about them or not.

C. LISTENING AND MAKING INFERENCES

Listen to each excerpt from the report. Then read the statement given. According to what the speaker says in the excerpt, how likely do you think he or she would be to agree with the statement? Circle the number on the scale. Compare your ratings with other students.

1. **Air Marshall A.K. Singh:** You see, it will initially start with people fighting for food and shelter. When the migration starts, every state would want to stop the migrations from happening. Eventually, it would have to become a military conflict. Which other means do you have to resolve your border issues?

   Statement: The military is the best organization to solve the conflicts presented by climate change.

   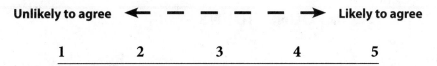

Unlikely to agree				Likely to agree
1	2	3	4	5

2. **Amanda Dory:** We don't anticipate that there are new mission areas as a result of climate change. Similarly, there may be changes in technical specifications for platforms, but not the need for new types of platforms that we don't already possess.

   Statement: The military will have to make big changes in preparation for climate change.

   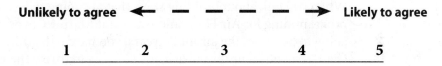

Unlikely to agree				Likely to agree
1	2	3	4	5

3. **Professor James Carafano:** These are big, huge, giant, complex systems, and people that take a linear approach to these things and say, "Oh, well, if this happens, then we're going to have to worry about that." That's not how reality works out.

   Statement: We can easily predict how climate change will affect us.

   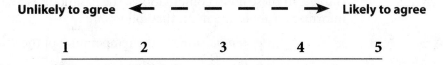

Unlikely to agree				Likely to agree
1	2	3	4	5

4. **Tom Gjelten, NPR News:** The bottom line: It's the job of national security officials at least to imagine future climate and security scenarios, whether they can do something about them or not.

   Statement: National security officials will be able to solve climate and security problems.

   Unlikely to agree ⬅ — — — — ➡ Likely to agree

1	2	3	4	5

IV. LOOKING AT LANGUAGE

A. USAGE: COMPOUND NOUNS

Notice Listen to the excerpts from the report. Notice the boldfaced nouns. How are these words formed?

Excerpt 1

So, it's that sort of **mindset,** I think, that has convinced, in my view, the vast majority of military leaders that **climate change** is a real threat and that the military plays an important role in confronting it.

Excerpt 2

When you talk about building ships that are going to last from 30 to 50 years or programming for Air Force and Navy and Marine Corps **aircraft** that are not going to be put in the air for 20 years, you have to be thinking about the kinds of changed conditions into which you're going to throw them in the future.

Explanation We often use two nouns together to express the meaning of one thing or person or idea.

   When two nouns are used together, we sometimes write them as one word, as in the above examples: ***mindset, aircraft***. These are called compound nouns.

   We also write compound nouns as two words, as in the above example: ***climate change***. In these noun combinations, the first noun is like an adjective. It gives information about the noun that follows.

   water temperature = the temperature of the water (in an ocean, lake)

   air pollution = contamination of air by smoke and harmful gases

   There are no rules for whether compound nouns are formed as two words or one. If you are in doubt, check your dictionary.

Exercise

Complete each sentence by making a compound noun with two words from the box. Decide whether the compound nouns should be written as one or two words. The first one has been done for you.

air	food	officials	threat
craft	~~forecasts~~	security	warning
Defense	House	shortages	watch
Department	intelligence	signs	~~weather~~
	list		White

1. Extreme weather patterns often make it difficult to give accurate

   weather forecasts .

2. There are not always enough _____ to give people time to prepare for major storms, hurricanes, or tornadoes.

3. Climate change is now viewed as a(n) _____ by some governments.

4. Climate change is not just the concern of the _____; the Pentagon is also involved.

5. The _____ is one of the branches of the government that is responsible for dealing with climate change in the United States

6. Like the military, _____ such as those who work in the C.I.A., consider climate change a threat.

7. The military predicts that there will be severe _____, which will lead to famine in some countries.

8. To prepare for climate change, the design of ships and _____ may need to change.

9. Countries that may become destabilized as a result of dramatic climate

   change are now on a(n) _____.

B. PRONUNCIATION: STRESS IN COMPOUND NOUNS

Notice   **Listen to the excerpts. Notice the boldfaced words. Which word (or syllable) is stressed in each compound noun?**

Excerpt 1

So, it's that sort of **mindset**, I think, that has convinced, in my view, the vast majority of military leaders that **climate change** is a real threat and that the military plays an important role in confirming it.

Excerpt 2

When you talk about building ships that are going to last from 30 to 50 years or programming for Air Force and Navy and Marine Corps **aircraft** that are not going to be put in the air for 20 years, you have to be thinking about the kinds of changed conditions into which you're going to throw them in the future.

Explanation   As you noticed in the section above, compound nouns are formed by combining two nouns. Sometimes the nouns are joined together as one word. Sometimes they remain separate.

In compound nouns, the first noun is more heavily stressed than the second noun. It is also pronounced with a higher pitch.

In *mindset*, *mind* is given more stress and a higher pitch than *set*.

In *climate change*, *climate* is given more stress and a higher pitch than *change*.

In *aircraft*, *air* is given more stress and a higher pitch than *craft*.

Exercise

Work in pairs. For items 1–5, write the correct responses from the box to complete the mini-dialogues. Then choose A and B roles and read the dialogues aloud. Be sure to read the compound nouns with the correct stress and pitch.

> Actually, there aren't. We just have better **sensor technology** to detect them.
>
> It's not the same. You will be surprised to see how **beach erosion** is changing the whole **coastline**.
>
> Yes. It's because the polar **ice caps** are melting!
>
> They're putting **sandbags** there to stop the river from flooding.
>
> We have had less **snowfall** in the winter and more **heat waves** in the summer.

1. A: Why are there so many people standing along the **riverbed**?

   B: _____

2. A: I'm hoping to spend some time at the **seashore** this summer.

   B: _____

3. A: What kinds of **weather extremes** have you experienced where you live?

   B: _____

4. A: There seem to be more **earthquakes** around the world every year!

   B: _____

5. A: Can you explain why **sea levels** are rising?

   B: _____

Repeat the same procedure for items 6–10. Change roles when you read the mini-dialogues.

> Some of them were started by **lightning strikes**, but many of them were started by human beings!
>
> People are proposing to build a better **sea wall**.
>
> The **Gulf Stream**, the **surface current** driven by the **Trade Winds,** could be disturbed. It's what brings warm weather to Europe.
>
> There can be serious **runoff**, or even **landslides**, when water is not absorbed by the soil.
>
> Well, it sure seems to me that **thunderclaps** are louder, and **lightning bolts** are more frequent.

6. A: Do you think **thunderstorms** have become more violent in recent years?

   B: _____

7. A: How might **ocean currents** cause Europe to have a colder climate in the future?

   B: _____

8. A: What happens when there is a lot of **rainfall** after a long, dry period?

   B: _____

9. A: Why have there been so many **wildfires** this year?

   B: _____

10. A: What is the best method of **flood control** for this coastal area?

   B: _____

C. DISCOURSE ANALYSIS: JARGON

Notice Listen to the excerpt from the report. Why does the reporter have to explain what Ms. Dory is talking about?

Excerpt

Amanda Dory: We don't anticipate that there are new mission areas as a result of climate change. Similarly, there may be changes in technical specifications for platforms, but not the need for new types of platforms that we don't already possess.

Tom Gjelten: In Pentagon jargon, platforms are the things on which weapons are carried, like ships or aircraft.

Explanation When people work in a particular field, such as the military, or when they share a common interest, they tend to develop a specialized vocabulary to express ideas easily between the members of the same group. This special set of words is called *jargon*. Jargon makes communication among groups more efficient, but it can also cause communication problems for people who are outside of the field. Jargon can confuse people, or it can cause people to feel like "outsiders."

In the example above, the interviewer explains to radio listeners what Dory means by the word "platform." He assumes that most of us will not understand the meaning of this word in the military context.

Exercise

Work in groups. All professions have their own jargon. Match the professional fields on the left with the examples of jargon from the field. Talk about what you think the words and phrases mean. Use a dictionary if necessary.

Professional Fields	Jargon
_____ 1. business	a. "risk-free trial" "target marketing" "mass mailing"
_____ 2. computers	b. "collateral damage" "fatigues" "friendly fire"
_____ 3. advertising	c. "touch base" "monetize" "win-win situation"
_____ 4. banking	d. "press release" "headline" "human-interest story"
_____ 5. broadcasting	e. "bounce back" "heart bypass" "meds"
_____ 6. legal	f. "lawsuit" "hung jury" "ruling"

___	7. medical	g.	"mainstream" "gifted students" "lesson plan"
___	8. military	h.	"url" "hyperlink" "html"
___	9. NASA	i.	"countdown" "all systems go" "liftoff"
___	10. news media	j.	"time out" "home run" "touchdown"
___	11. sports	l.	"tune in" "mic" "anchor"
___	12. teaching	m.	"withdrawal" "overdraft protection" "deposit"

V. FOLLOW-UP ACTIVITIES

A. DISCUSSION QUESTIONS

Work in groups. Discuss your answers to the questions.

1. Do you believe that the military should play a strong role in dealing with climate change? Is it the most appropriate organization to deal with climate change?

2. Can we predict climate-change scenarios and plan for the future? Do you agree that predicting the outcomes of climate change could be as dangerous as ignoring climate change?

B. CASE STUDY: CHICAGO'S PREPARATION FOR CLIMATE CHANGE

1. Take Notes to Prepare

In this report, you learned that climate change is now seen as a national security threat in both the United States and India.

Listen to the report again. Complete the notes about the military and intelligence officials' views on climate change and its effects on human life. Main topics and some examples have been provided for you. Use your notes to help you evaluate the case study that follows.

Government organizations concerned about climate change:

- *The White House and environmental officials* _____

- *The Pentagon* _____

- _____

- _____

Possible results of climate change:

- *melting of the Himalayan glaciers*

- _____

- _____

- *mass migrations across national borders*

- _____

- _____

- *violent conflicts over resources*

The Pentagon's predictions:

- *more severe weather events (in intensity and frequency)*

- _____

- _____

- *not new mission areas, but changes in technical specifications*

Security predictions related to climate change:

- _____

- _____

2. Consider the Issue

You have listened to some government (military and intelligence) concerns about climate change and how it may affect life in the future.

Read the case.

A few summers ago, 739 people died in Chicago from a heat wave that lasted a week. That number was more than double the number of people who died in the famous Great Chicago Fire of 1871. In the last three years, Chicago has experienced two of its most severe storms in the last 100 years, with up to 70-mile-per-hour winds. This heat wave and severe storms appear to be consistent with climate change. Predictions for Chicago's future are that its climate will resemble that of the much hotter Deep South within several decades.

Inspired by the famous Kyoto Conference, in which leaders from around the world agreed to make changes to greenhouse emissions, the former mayor of Chicago decided to make his city a model for climate change preparation. City officials examined the changes in Chicago's climate over the last century and found some disturbing data. If trends continue the way they have been going, Chicago will have a much hotter climate in the summer, a snowier climate in the winter, and a wetter climate in the spring. For example, in the 20th century, the city had an average of less than 15 days with temperatures over 90 degrees Fahrenheit (32°C). By the end of this century, it is predicted that there will be as many as 72 days with those temperatures. By 2070, 35 percent more rain is expected to fall in winter and spring, but 20 percent less rain is expected to fall in summer and fall. By then, Chicago will have changed its agricultural growing areas several times.

By 2050, Chicago's goal is to reach greenhouse emissions that are 80 percent below what they were in 1990. Today, the city is making major changes to its infrastructure as it prepares for extreme climate changes. Here are some examples of its ambitious goals:

<u>Tree planting</u>: The city is planting a million more trees, as trees provide shade and can improve air quality by absorbing carbon dioxide (CO_2). Chicago is also taking the six most common tree species off its planting list, as they will suffer from disease in a warmer climate. These trees will be replaced with heartier trees that can survive in much hotter temperatures, such as the swamp white oak and bald cypress, which currently grow in the Deep South.

<u>Paved streets and sidewalks</u>: Blacktop, the material typically used to build roads, absorbs heat as it attracts the sun and absorbs water. New materials are being used to pave streets, parking lots, and sidewalks. These materials reflect light, drain water for reuse, and expand in heat to prevent cracking. The city has already remade 150 small streets with this material, allowing 80 percent rainwater to pass through to the ground below. This reduces flooding.

<u>Improve transportation</u>: The city will improve walking and bike paths. The goal is for residents to walk or ride a bike for 5 percent of all trips less than 5 miles. Five hundred bike paths will be built so that every resident in Chicago will live within a half mile of a bike path. The city hopes to increase the number of bike-transit trips by 10 percent per year.

<u>The electric car</u>: To help reduce energy consumption and greenhouse gas emissions, Chicago has a $2-million plan to lead the way in developing electric cars. With 280 charging stations around the city, two of which will be solar-powered, Chicagoans will be encouraged to buy battery-powered vehicles.

<u>Garden rooftops</u>: This project gets nature and industry to work together effectively. The city plans to add 6,000 gardens to its city rooftops. The rooftops will reduce air pollution by absorbing more carbon dioxide. They will also reduce heating and air conditioning costs. Moreover, they last longer than standard roofs.

Of course there are some criticisms of these projects. What if the climate change predictions are wrong? Who will pay for all the changes in Chicago's infrastructure? Who will profit from these changes? Could any of these changes actually increase the problem of climate change rather than solve it? Consider these questions as you evaluate the usefulness of Chicago's solutions for your city.

3. Role-play

Work in groups. Act as a committee that is studying cities' plans for dealing with climate change in the future. Discuss the pros and cons of Chicago's plan and whether they would work in your city. Make a list of recommendations for your city. Then share them with the class.

"Preparing for Climate Change" was first broadcast on Morning Edition, *December 14, 2009. The reporter is Tom Gjelten.*

Everybody Is an Above-Average Driver

I. ANTICIPATING THE ISSUE

Discuss your answers to the questions.

1. From the title and picture, what do you think the interview in this unit is about?

2. Do you drive? If so, do you think you are an above-average, average, or below-average driver? (If you don't drive, answer this question for the person who drives you most often.)

3. In your opinion, what are the biggest issues that involve driving and traffic today?

Exercise 1

Label each part of the drawing with the correct word or phrase from the box.

crosswalk	right-of-way
intersection	roundabout
oncoming traffic	T-bone collision
pedestrian	

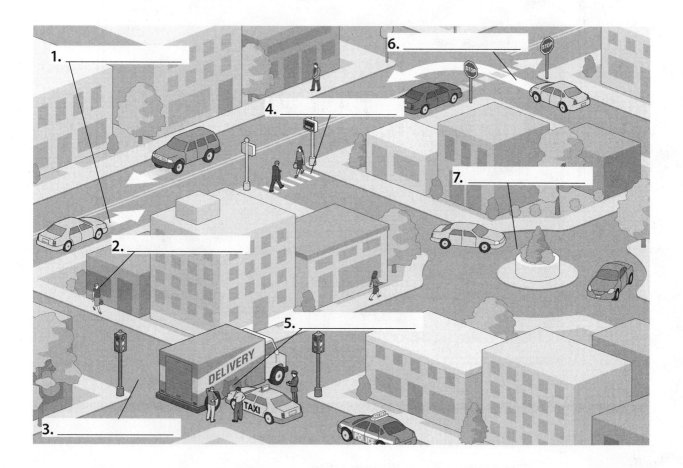

1. _____

6. _____

4. _____

7. _____

2. _____

5. _____

3. _____

Exercise 2

Read the mini-dialogues. Use the context to help you understand the meaning of the boldfaced words and phrases. Then circle the letter of the response that best fits the dialogue.

1. A: The car in front of me keeps speeding up and slowing down. It's driving me crazy!

   B: I know. Some drivers have pretty strange **quirks**.

   A: _____
      a. Yeah, he really needs a new car. That one's so old!
      b. I know. Look at that woman putting on makeup while she's driving!

2. A: Look at all these cars!

   B: Don't worry. There's just some construction ahead.

   A: Yeah. But I hate driving in so much traffic. It **unnerves** me.

   B: _____
      a. Yeah, I prefer to drive myself.
      b. Me, too. I feel stressed when the roads are crowded.

3. A: Dad, I'm sorry to tell you that I hit another car while backing out in the parking lot today.

   B: From now on, you've got to be more **vigilant**!

   A: _____
      a. OK. I'll tell you sooner next time.
      b. You're right. I promise I'll be more careful in the future.

4. A: I find it hard to drive the same road back and forth to work each day.

   B: Why? Does your mind **wander** and keep you from focusing on the road?

   A: _____
      a. Yes, I'm usually thinking about my work or my kids.
      b. Yes, listening to music usually helps.

5. A: What's the biggest **distraction** for you while driving on the highway?

   B: I don't know, . . . probably all the signs and billboards.

   A: _____
      a. I agree. They do help make the roads safer.
      b. I know, sometimes I look at them and then realize I've driven out of my lane!

6. A: There are too many traffic accidents these days!

   B: I know. And, unfortunately, most of them happen for **mundane** reasons, like looking at a pedestrian.

   A: _____
   a. I disagree. It's those people who text while driving that cause the most accidents!
   b. Yes, I've heard that most accidents happen very close to home.

7. A: I think the rain is turning to sleet. The roads feel a bit slippery.

   B: Oh, no. That's a real **hazard**.

   A: _____
   a. I know. I'll be careful.
   b. You're right. It's not sleet. It's still raining.

8. A: Did you forget where you were going?

   B: Yeah, sorry. I was **absentmindedly** driving us home.

   A: _____
   a. You really need to pay more attention.
   b. I'm glad to know you're driving carefully.

9. A: Don't you think it's time for the governments in all countries to **legislate** "no texting while driving"?

   B: _____
   a. Why? Do you think the policy doesn't work?
   b. It's a great idea, but no one follows the law anyway.

10. A: I hate getting stuck in traffic like this! I can't focus.

    B: Why? Does it cause you to **daydream**?

    A: _____
    a. No, I never fall asleep at the wheel!
    b. Yes, I start thinking about my dinner plans and forget that I'm driving.

11. A: Look at David up ahead! He's driving too fast for these road conditions.

    B: I know. He's from a warm climate and has probably never gotten any **feedback** to know how to drive in snow.

    A: _____
    a. He'll learn to slow down if he hits a patch of ice!
    b. You're right. He is a very experienced driver.

12. A: Why is that motorcycle rider driving so fast? Look, he's weaving through lanes of traffic! Doesn't he realize he could cause an accident?

    B: He must have a problem with **overconfidence**.

    A: _____
    a. I guess he thinks other drivers will do the right thing.
    b. I guess he thinks he should drive more carefully.

13. A: I saw an accident the other day. Both drivers got out of their cars and started screaming at each other.

    B: Why? Because neither was willing to **own up to** the fact that he was in the wrong?

    A: _____
    a. Sometimes people just can't admit their own mistakes.
    b. Yes, they both knew that they were wrong.

III. LISTENING

A. LISTENING FOR MAIN IDEAS

Listen to the interview. After each of the five parts, you will hear a beep. Answer the question in a complete sentence. Then compare your answers with those of another student.

Part 1   According to Tom Vanderbilt, what has improved in driving?

_____

_____

Part 2   In which types of situations does Vanderbilt say drivers "tend to act more cautiously"?

_____

_____

Part 3   What does Vanderbilt say is a major cause of driver error and car crashes?

_____

_____

Part 4

According to one study, what is one of the strangest reasons for distraction?

_____

_____

Part 5

What does Vanderbilt say most people feel about their own driving?

_____

_____

B. LISTENING FOR DETAILS

Read the statements for Part 1. Then listen to Part 1 again and write *T* (true) or *F* (false). Compare your answers with those of another student. If your answers are different, listen again.

Part 1

_____ 1. Americans are driving more than usual this week.

_____ 2. New technologies have not reduced traffic deaths.

_____ 3. People have become safer drivers.

Repeat the same procedure for Parts 2–5.

Part 2

_____ 4. Human beings have evolved to move faster.

_____ 5. Vanderbilt thinks our perception of risk does not match reality.

_____ 6. According to Tom Vanderbilt, roundabouts are circles of death.

_____ 7. The most dangerous move in traffic is a left turn against oncoming traffic.

_____ 8. Roundabouts have good signs and symbols to help people drive.

_____ 9. Vanderbilt believes that stress helps people drive more safely.

_____ 10. Vanderbilt says large, organized intersections cause T-bone collisions.

_____ 11. Pedestrians in crosswalks have the same right-of-way as cars with green lights.

Part 3

_____ 12. Cameras in cars give important data about distraction.

_____ 13. Until now, no one suspected distraction was a cause of driver error.

_____ 14. According to Vanderbilt, we never really become good at driving.

_____ 15. Driving dulls the mind.

_____ 16. The mind is usually 100 percent occupied when driving.

Part 4

_____ 17. Texting is called the "perfect storm of distraction" because it involves many senses.

_____ 18. Vanderbilt feels that cell phones are the number one distraction.

_____ 19. Carmakers do not understand the danger of radios.

_____ 20. It would be easy to legislate absentminded driving.

_____ 21. Humans should be expected to maintain 100 percent vigilance.

Part 5

_____ 22. The story by Bonnie Joe Campbell illustrates how easy it is to become distracted while driving.

_____ 23. Vanderbilt had an accident because of a radio.

_____ 24. Vanderbilt got feedback at age 16.

_____ 25. Vanderbilt says that a lack of feedback leads to drivers' overconfidence.

_____ 26. Many people admit that they are below-average drivers.

C. LISTENING AND MAKING INFERENCES

Listen to the excerpts from the interview and circle the best answers. Compare your answers with those of other students.

1. Why does the interviewer ask this question?
   a. He is surprised by what Tom Vanderbilt said.
   b. He didn't hear what Vanderbilt said.
   c. His own experience supports what Vanderbilt said.

2. Why does the interviewer laugh here?
   a. It's funny that public radio would be considered mundane.
   b. Children don't listen to the radio.
   c. Vanderbilt is complimenting his radio program.

3. How does the story fit Vanderbilt's research?
   a. It explains how bad weather can cause accidents.
   b. It shows how easy it is to be distracted while driving.
   c. It illustrates how accidents can be caused by children.

A. USAGE: SUPERLATIVE FORMS

Notice   Listen to the following excerpt from the interview. What do you notice about the grammatical forms of the three underlined examples?

Excerpt

What are some of the things that can distract me in a car or that I may allow to distract myself in the car, that are <u>not too bad</u>, and some that are <u>a little worse</u> and <u>the very worst</u>?

Explanation   The adjectives listed in the example are formed with an adjective (*bad*), its irregular comparative form (*worse*), and its irregular superlative form (*worst*). Note that the superlative is formed with the article "the."

Here are the ways we form superlative adjectives:

1. If the adjective is short (one syllable or two syllables ending in -*y*), we use:

   the + adjective + *est*

   the loudest car   *the foggiest road*

2. If the adjective is long (two or more syllables), we use:

   the most / the least + adjective

   the most dangerous moves   *the least distracted drivers*

3. There are some adjectives that have irregular superlative forms:

   the best drivers   *the worst roads*

Here is a list of common irregular comparisons of adjectives:

Adjective	Comparative	Superlative
bad	worse	the worst
far	farther / further	the farthest / furthest
good	better	the best
little	less	the least
many / a lot of	more	the most
much / a lot of	more	the most

Exercise

Read the text describing a famous Walt Disney cartoon. Fill in the blanks with the superlative forms of the adjectives in parentheses. Note that some of the superlatives are irregular.

In 1950, Walt Disney produced one of _____1_____ (good) examples of what happens to people when they get behind the wheel of a car: _____2_____ (kindly) person can become _____3_____ (nasty) person when he or he is driving on the road!

In *Motor Mania*, Mr. Walker, _____4_____ (nice) man in the neighborhood, becomes Mr. Wheeler, _____5_____ (thoughtless) driver on the highway. He thinks he owns the road. He drives through town, yelling at other drivers, and crashing into anything in his path.

He is one of _____6_____ (high) paying taxpayers in the county, so he thinks he should be able to use the highway as he wishes. When he decides to go on a leisurely drive down the road, making all the cars behind him drive at _____7_____ (slow) speed possible, it is clear that he enjoys feeling in control. Drivers accuse him of being _____8_____ (big) road hog on the road. And when he approaches a red light and must wait 30 seconds for the light to turn green, he acts as though he is _____9_____ (impatient)

driver of all of the drivers on the highway. Moreover, when he tries to park his car in tight spaces, he exhibits _____ (bad) form of parking,
10

crashing into the car in front of him, as well as the car behind him in order to park his car.

At the end of the cartoon, Mr. Wheeler becomes Mr. Walker again. He is now _____ (cautious) pedestrian on the street, looking both
11

ways and waiting for the light. He has great difficulty crossing the street because of all the terrible drivers. But once he makes it through the intersection in the difficult traffic, he protects himself by jumping back into the protective armor of his car: his _____ (safe) refuge. But because his car is
12

no longer functioning, he must have his car pulled away by a tow truck. Here, Mr. Wheeler exhibits _____ (angry) feelings he has about
13

not being in control behind the wheel as he yells, "Ah, shut up" to the narrator, who tries to teach him a lesson in good driver behavior. Mr. Wheeler may be _____ (less) able of all of us to learn the lesson of good driving.
14

B. PRONUNCIATION: THE *TH* SOUNDS /θ/ AND /ð/

Notice **Listen to the excerpt. How are the underlined words pronounced?**

Excerpt

What are some of the things that can distract me in a car or that I may allow to distract myself in the car, that are not too bad, and some that are a little worse and the very worst?

Explanation The underlined words in the excerpt contains the sounds /θ/ (things) and /ð/ (that, the), which require placing the tongue tip between the front teeth. These sounds are sometimes hard for students to pronounce, especially if they do not have similar sounds in their own language. Some students might feel embarrassed by having to stick out their tongue to produce these sounds. However, when the *th* sounds are not pronounced correctly, it can have a negative effect on native English listeners.

The /ð/ sound in the word *the* is voiced, like in the words *that*, *there*, and *then*. English words that use /θ/ are unvoiced, such as in the words *things*, *through*, and *thick*.

Exercise 1

Work in pairs. Go back to the exercise in Part A. Underline the words with the *th* sounds. Then take turns reading paragraphs of the story. Focus on the pronunciation of *th*.

Exercise 2

Work in pairs. Read the list of idioms and expressions with *th* sounds. Check their meanings with your teacher or with a dictionary.

through thick and thin

Where there's thunder, there's lightning.

think it through

this, that, and the other

north and south

soothes the soul

smooth things over

weather thermometer

thousands of thoroughfares

thick as thieves

Exercise 3

Work with your partner. Complete the sentences with the best idiom or expression from Exercise 2. Then take turns reading the sentences aloud, focusing on the *th* sounds.

1. We heard a loud crack in the sky and said "_____

   _____." So we decided not to drive home.

2. My GPS seemed to be directing me in the wrong direction, so I stopped

   driving in order to _____: Should I follow these directions
   or go with my own instincts?

3. The highway traffic was heavy going both _____. We knew it
   was going to be a long drive.

4. Jack and his friends piled into the car and drove off to spend the weekend together, feeling _____.

5. Tom glanced out his window at the _____ to see if it was warm enough to drive out to the lake for a swim.

6. When she ran out of gas on the highway, Heather decided to call her brother for help. He was always there for her _____.

7. Joe had a serious argument with his coworker in the office, so when he got home, he decided to drive over to his place to _____.

8. Some people like to get in their cars and drive when they're having a difficult day. For them, driving _____.

9. With its huge geographic area and its strong car culture, America is known as the nation of _____.

10. When people get stuck in traffic, their minds often wander, thinking about _____.

C. DISCOURSE ANALYSIS: SPEED OF DELIVERY

Notice Listen to the interviewee's first comment in the interview. What can you say about the way he speaks? Why do you think he speaks this way?

Excerpt

Human nature is always really the X factor in this, because where the gains have really come from, in my opinion, is simply cars have become safer and the roads have been made safer. I don't think there's been a qualitative improvement in the way people are driving.

Explanation Speakers may alter their speed of delivery for different reasons. If they feel pressure to express their ideas in a short amount of time, such as in radio call-in shows, they may speak more quickly. They may also speak fast if they feel anxious about speaking in front of an audience, such as when politicians deliver a difficult message. Speakers may also speak more quickly if they fear being interrupted by the person with whom they are speaking. A fast speed of delivery is more common in spontaneous conversation than it is in prepared speech.

Listeners may have problems listening to a speaker if the speed of delivery is too fast or too slow. They may lose the message or stop listening if the delivery is too fast; they may feel bored or tune out if the delivery is too slow.

Exercise 1

Work in pairs. Take turns giving one-minute speeches about the following topics. Deliver the first one-minute speech, using a slow speed of delivery. For the second mini-speech, deliver your speech using a very fast speed of delivery.

<u>Mini-speech 1</u> (slow)
Student A
which driver behaviors annoy you

<u>Mini-speech 2</u> (fast)
Student A
where you like / don't like to drive

Student B
your opinion of traffic laws

Student B
what the worst driver distractions are

Exercise 2

Discuss the effects of speed of delivery of the two speeches. How did speed of delivery affect your interest in listening to your partner?

V. FOLLOW-UP ACTIVITIES

A. DISCUSSION QUESTIONS

Work in groups. Discuss your answers to the questions.

1. Do you agree with Tom Vanderbilt that most people consider themselves to be above-average drivers? Why are people unwilling to admit that they might be below-average drivers?

2. What kinds of situations make you fearful in traffic? Which type of driver behavior makes you the most uncomfortable?

3. How has driving changed in recent years? Do you agree with Vanderbilt that cars and roads have improved, but drivers have not?

B. ORAL PRESENTATION: INTERNATIONAL TRAFFIC PROBLEMS

1. Take Notes to Prepare

Focusing on the problems drivers face in today's world will help you prepare your oral presentation for the exercise that follows.

Listen to the report again. Take notes on the issues that drivers face in today's world. Main topics and an example have been provided for you. Use your notes to help you prepare for your own oral presentation on driving / traffic issues in another country.

Improvements in driving:

cars safer

_____

_____

What unnerves drivers:

_____

_____

Distractions that can cause car crashes:

_____

_____

_____

_____

Problems with drivers:

_____

_____

_____

2. Prepare Your Presentation

Prepare a five-minute oral presentation. Choose a country with which you are familiar. Use the Internet to research the current driving and traffic issues of that country and take notes on your findings.

You may want to research the following information:

- fatality statistics (number of deaths caused by car accidents each year)
- new safety devices that have been introduced to cars
- new traffic laws (cell phone use, texting while driving, etc.)
- drunk driving statistics and solutions
- aging drivers
- changes in society because of cars and driving (when children go to school, when meetings are held, when people shop, etc.)

Follow the Oral Presentation Procedures below.

Oral Presentation Procedures

1. Summarize your research findings on an index card. You will refer to these notes when you give your presentation.

2. Create three to five PowerPoint slides to enhance your talk. Keep the text very brief. Use more images to support your presentation.

3. Practice your presentation at home. Give your presentation in front of friends or family members, or in front of the mirror. Time yourself for no more than five minutes.

4. Give your five-minute presentation in class. Be sure to include an introduction to the country you have chosen and its current traffic issues. Present the data you have collected. Conclude with your own opinion. Discuss whether or not you think the country is dealing well with its traffic problems.

5. Follow the points in the box on page 174. Your teacher or classmates may want to rate your presentation according to content interest, organization, pronunciation, fluency, grammar, and vocabulary.

Useful Points for Oral Presentations

When you make an oral presentation, consider the following:

1. Present a brief outline of your talk in the introduction. Give the audience a general overview of your talk.

2. Provide handouts for the audience.

3. Ask rhetorical questions, i.e., questions which engage the audience's listening but which are not to be answered. For example, "So why has traffic increased so much in recent years? It is because . . . "

4. Look at the audience. Check your notes or briefly point out information on PowerPoint slides, if needed, but always look at the audience when you speak.

"Everybody is an Above-Average Driver" was first broadcast on Morning Edition, *November 25, 2009. The interviewer is Steve Inskeep.*

NOTES

NOTES

NOTES

NOTES

NOTES